The Thinking Tree

MYTHOLOGICAL CREATURES
& LEGENDARY ANIMALS

A Multi Subject Homeschooling Journal

MYTHOLOGY, HISTORY, SOCIAL STUDIES, CREATIVE WRITING, COMICS, POETRY, DRAWING & GEOGRAPHY

DISCLAIMER:
SOME OF THESE CREATURES MAY NOT BE MYTHS, BUT THEY ARE ALL LEGENDARY. YOU CAN DECIDE FOR YOURSELF IF THEY ARE REAL OR IMAGINED.

PARENTS/TEACHERS:

Due to the content of this book, it is up to your discretion to decide whether or not the student can do outside research.

Looking in library books or online is not necessary, but our recommendation is for the student to have parental guidance at all times when researching this topic.

The poems are meant to be informative, and the origin of each creature can be found in the Table of Contents page at the beginning of the book.

ABOUT THE ARTWORK:

We chose two talented teen artists to illustrate this book. They both have their own unique styles and did their own research about what the creature looks might like. We hope you enjoy seeing the differences in each artist's interpretation. Kaylea drew the coloring pages, Quinn drew the mazes.
How would you draw each creature?

FUNSCHOOLING.COM

THE CREATURES

Loch Ness Monster of Scottish Folklore

Mngwa of Tanzania

Werewolf of Europe

Sleipnr of Norse Mythology

Medusa of Greek Mythology

Wolpertinger of German Folklore

Apep of Egyptian Theology

Capricorn of Greek Mythology

Enfield of Europe

Cyclops of Greek Mythology

Gnome of Scandinavia

Piasa Bird of Native American Mythology

Fairy of English Folklore

Dragon of Worminster Sleight of English Folklore

Mermaid of Assyrian Mythology

Centaur of Greek Mythology

Faun of Roman Mythology

Griffin of Greek Mythology

Phoenix of Greek Mythology

Unicorn of Greek Mythology

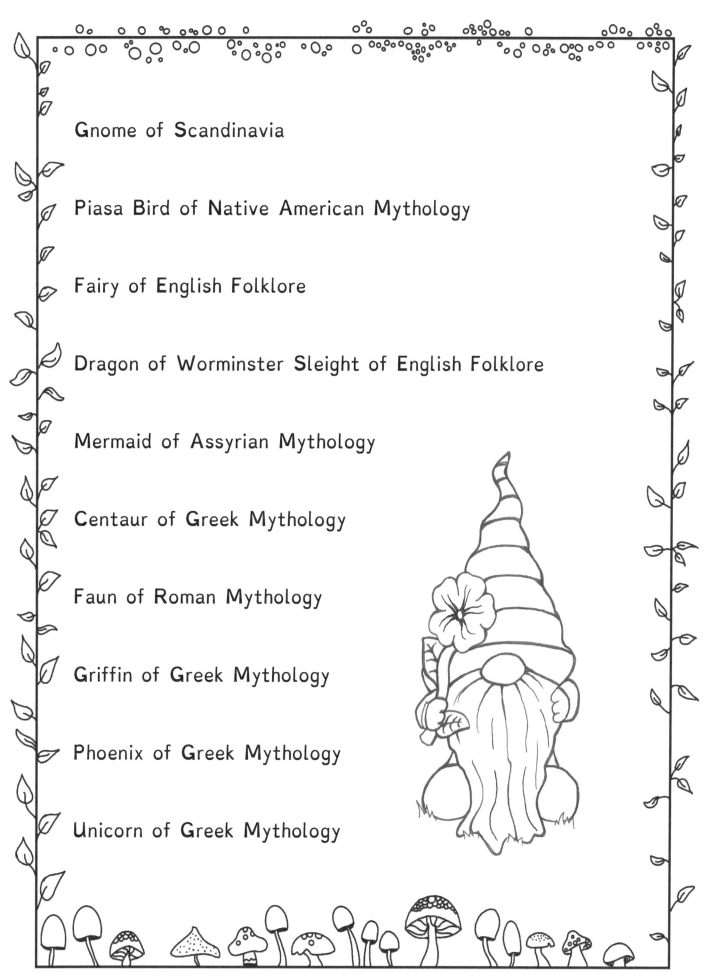

Elves of North Germanic Mythology

Nymph of Greek Mythology

Pixie of Celtic Mythology

Pegasus of Greek Mythology

Hydra of Greek Mythology

Leviathan of Hebrew Scriptures

Longma of Chinese Mythology

African Rainbow Serpent of Afrcian Mythology

Kitsune of Japanese Folklore

Midgard Wyrm of Norse Mythology

Cerberus of Greek Mythology

Oriental Dragon of the First Chinese Dynasty (Xia)

Nemean Lion of Greek Mythology

Bisterne Dragon of English Mythology

Fantasy Dragon of Any Origin

LOCH NESS MONSTER

Call me Loch, or Ness, or Nessie
But Monster's not my name
My history is muddled, messy
But that's just what comes with fame

Thousands of creatures undiscovered
And you think you have a chance?
Being hidden isn't hard
It's an easy thing, a dance!

And the scientists will tell you
(And your parents will insist)
That a creature as big and cool as me
Never could exist

But go yourself and spend some time
In the lake they said I'd be
And they might start calling you crazy too
For the things that you might see

CREATIVE WRITING

Write a short story about this creature.

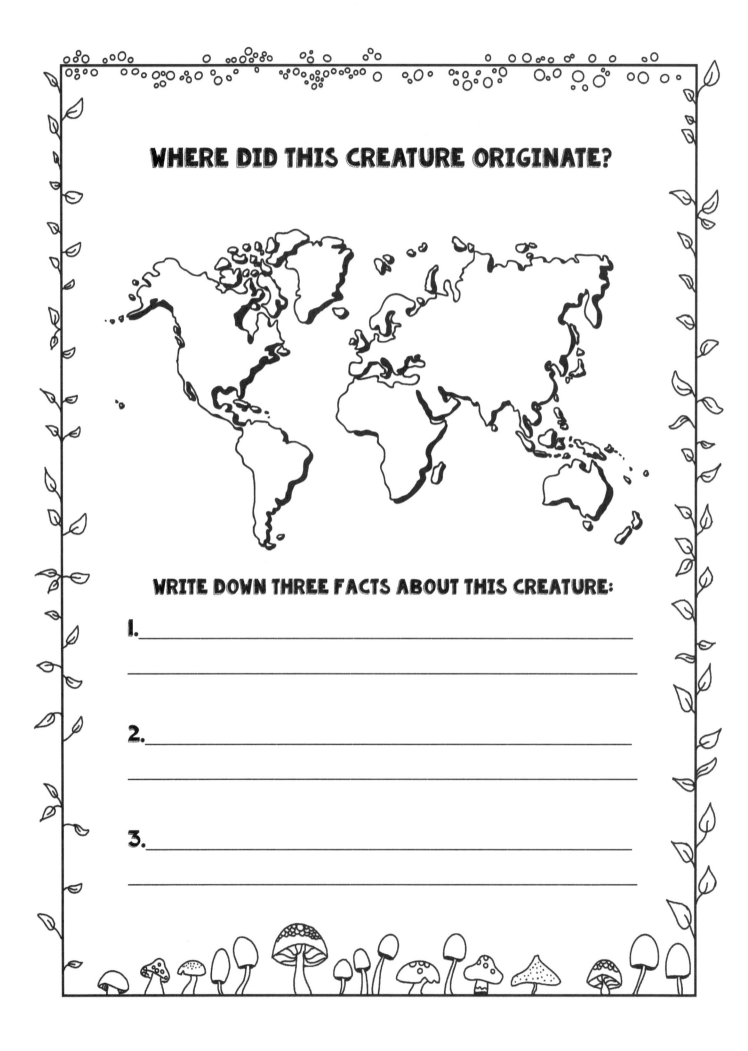

MNGWA

They call us the Mngwa!
The "strange ones", "bizarre"

They pass us off as leopards
But that isn't what we are

In truth we are much stronger
Than any bigger cat you know

We stalk our prey much quieter
We strike with single blows

And when we've caught our dinner
Like ghosts, we disappear

You'll never see us coming
And never know we're near

CREATIVE WRITING

Write a short story about this creature.

WHERE DID THIS CREATURE ORIGINATE?

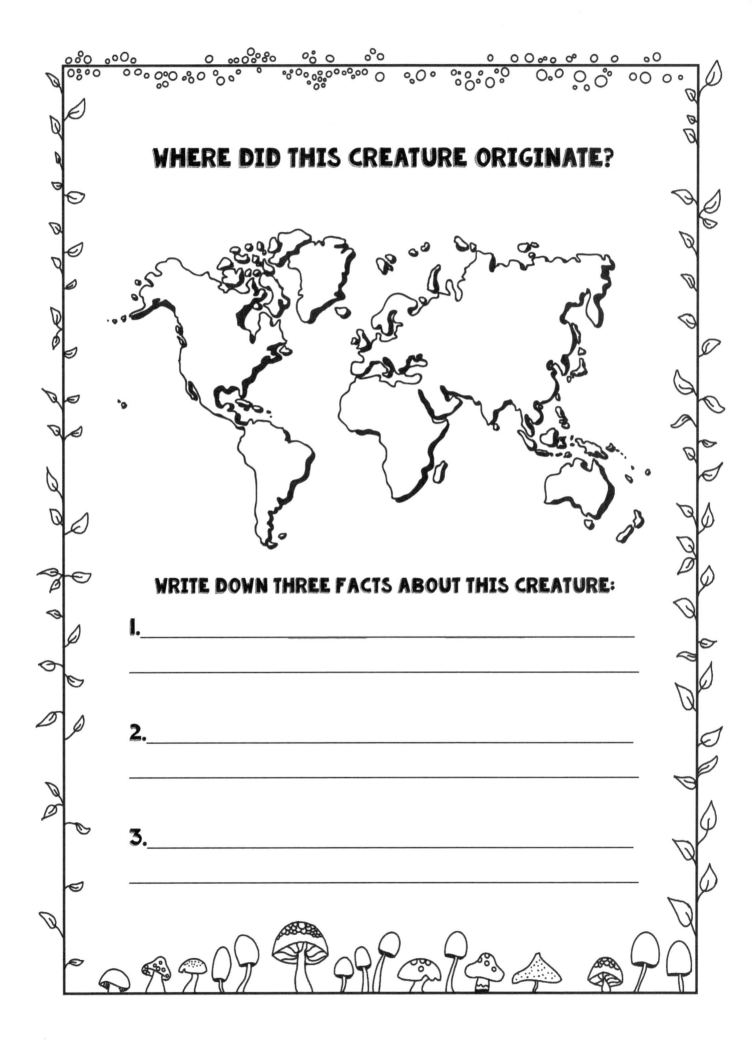

WRITE DOWN THREE FACTS ABOUT THIS CREATURE:

1._____
_____

2._____
_____

3._____
_____

WEREWOLF

Have you heard the Werewolf Legends?
When you did, were you afraid?
I'm not polite or generous
I always misbehave

I used to be a little boy
My mother taught me "thanks" and "please"
Then my father made a wolf pelt coat
And I turned into one of these

I'm frightening in all my ways
And I come out late at night
I find a clifftop, and let out a howl
When the moon is round and bright

Legend has it, I'm out there still
Weaving through the forest trees
And I used to be a little boy
Who once said "thanks" and "please"

DRAW THE MISSING PARTS

CREATIVE WRITING

Write a short story about this creature.

_____
_____
_____
_____
_____
_____
_____
_____
_____
_____
_____
_____
_____
_____
_____
_____

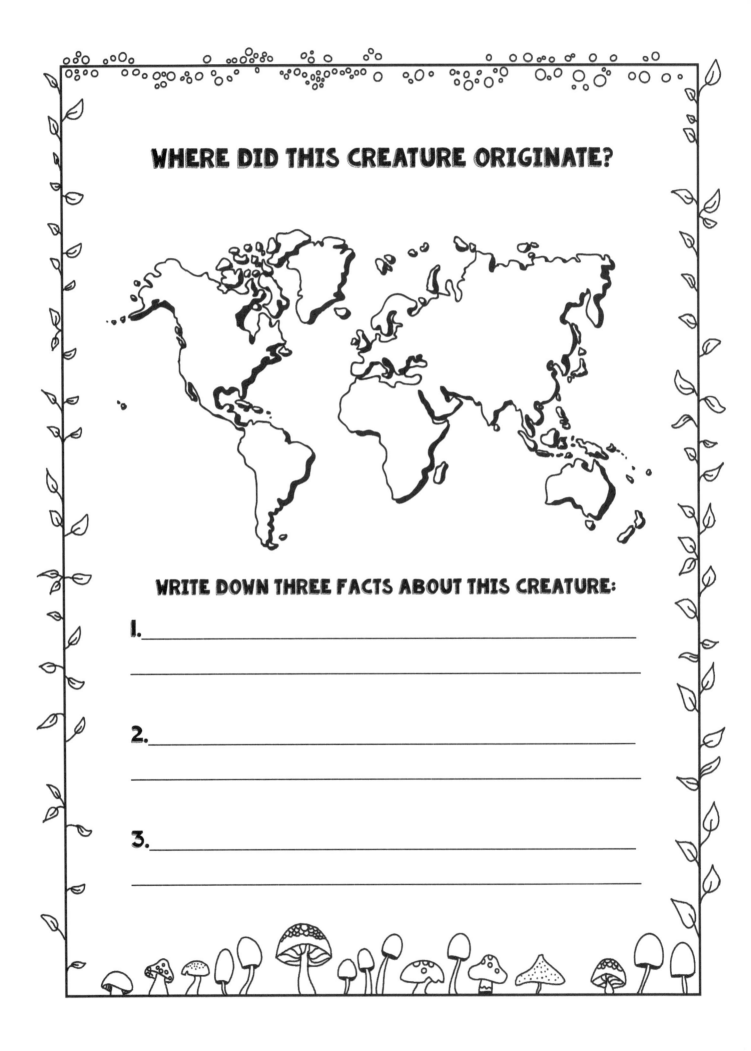

WHERE DID THIS CREATURE ORIGINATE?

WRITE DOWN THREE FACTS ABOUT THIS CREATURE:

1._____
_____

2._____
_____

3._____
_____

SLEIPNR

I am Sleipnr
Favorite mount of Odin
My eight legs
Move quickly
As I slip through the air

Traveling faster
Than wind
To get my master
To wherever
His Majesty should wish

I can run
Between realms
As easily as trotting to town

I am the fastest
Most cunning
Most dutiful steed
Mythology has ever seen

CREATIVE WRITING

Write a short story about this creature.

_____
_____
_____
_____
_____
_____
_____
_____
_____
_____
_____
_____
_____
_____
_____
_____
_____

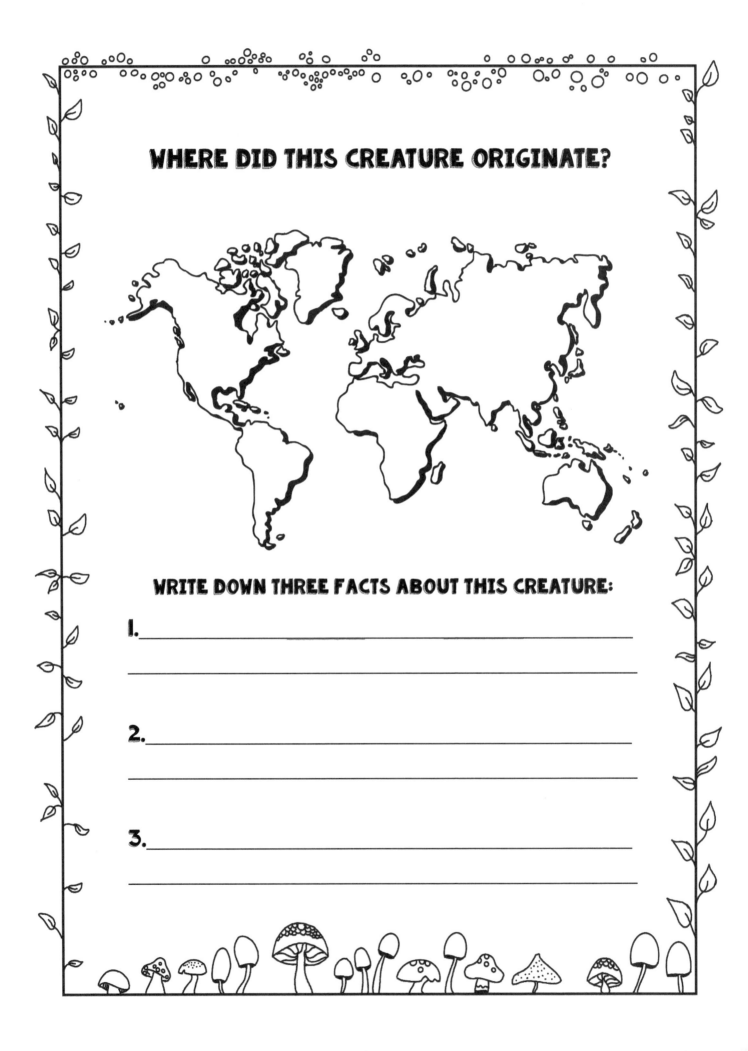

WHERE DID THIS CREATURE ORIGINATE?

WRITE DOWN THREE FACTS ABOUT THIS CREATURE:

1._____
_____

2._____
_____

3._____
_____

MEDUSA

My name means "protection"
And my figure rests upon
Flags and shields and emblems
My story's in your songs

Some depict me as a masterpiece
Some say that I am mad
That I'm the monster in your closet
And I'm only gross and bad

Am I the original Lady Liberty?
Or am I evil, rude and dark?
My hair is made of serpents
But am I really bad at heart?

I beg you to have pity
For the Gorgon that I am!
We all do good and bad things
But we do the best we can

So maybe I'm just trying
Just like everybody else
We make mistakes, we stumble
While we all better ourselves

CREATIVE WRITING

Write a short story about this creature.

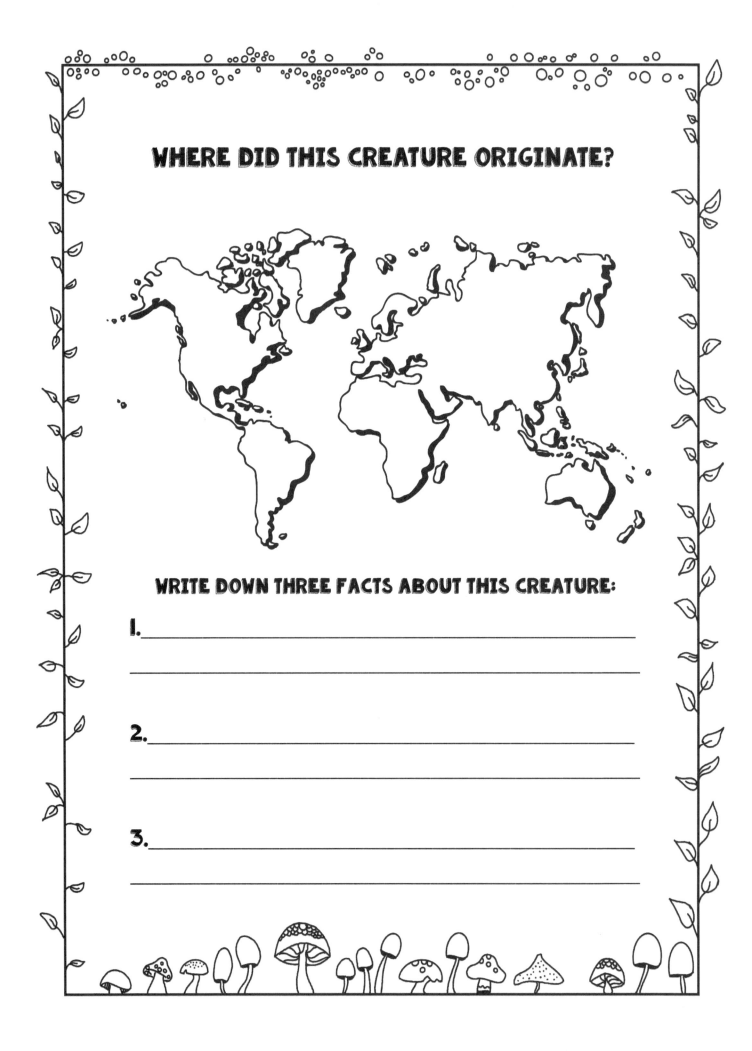

WOLPERTINGER

I'm the child of the Bavarian forest
Perhaps only a story, a fable, a legend

But if I really was out there
You'd find me in the hollows
Collecting herbs and roots
From the pine-needle floor

And if I really was out there
(And you really wanted to see me)
You would go out at night
And light a candle
I would follow the soft glow
Until I came to you

But look, and do not touch
Because if you do
You might just find yourself
Growing fur and sprouting wings
Until you have become
A Wolpertinger too

DRAW THE MISSING PARTS

CREATIVE WRITING

Write a short story about this creature.

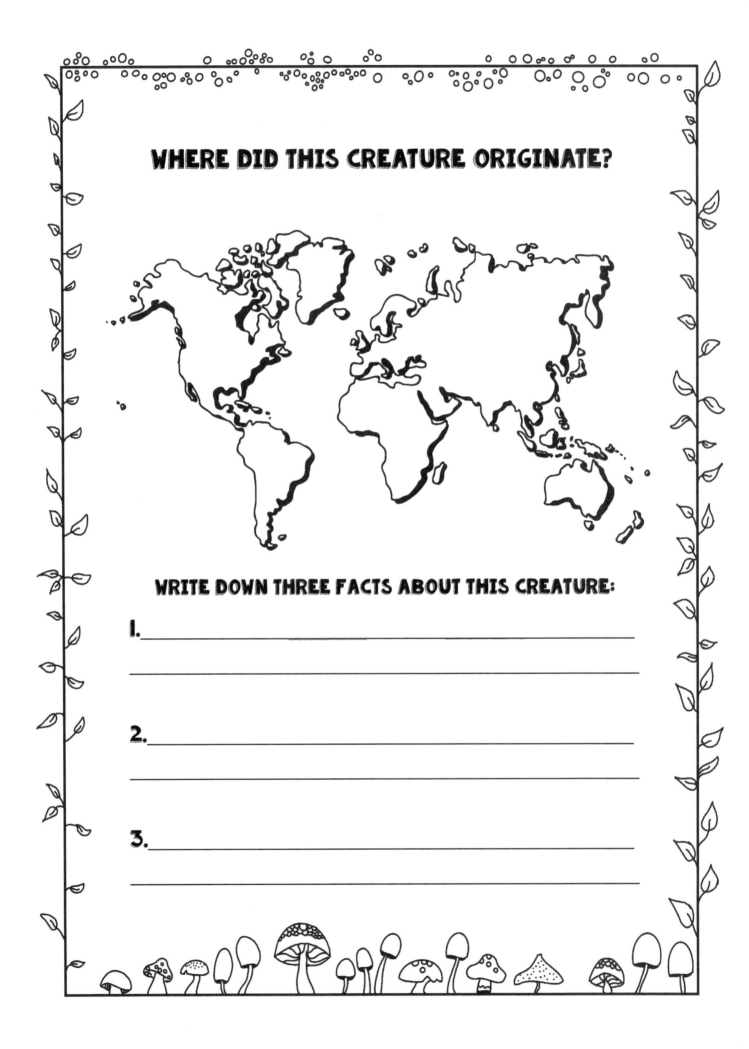

APEP

Look at me, I'm fifty feet!
I'm black, and orange
And green!

My name is Apep!
I am the king of the night
I battle the sun,
(and usually lose)

Unless we eclipse
And I claim the world
And block the sun
For one whole day

But don't be sad
He will be back
To light your homes
And warm your skin
When I am done
Casting your sky
With stars

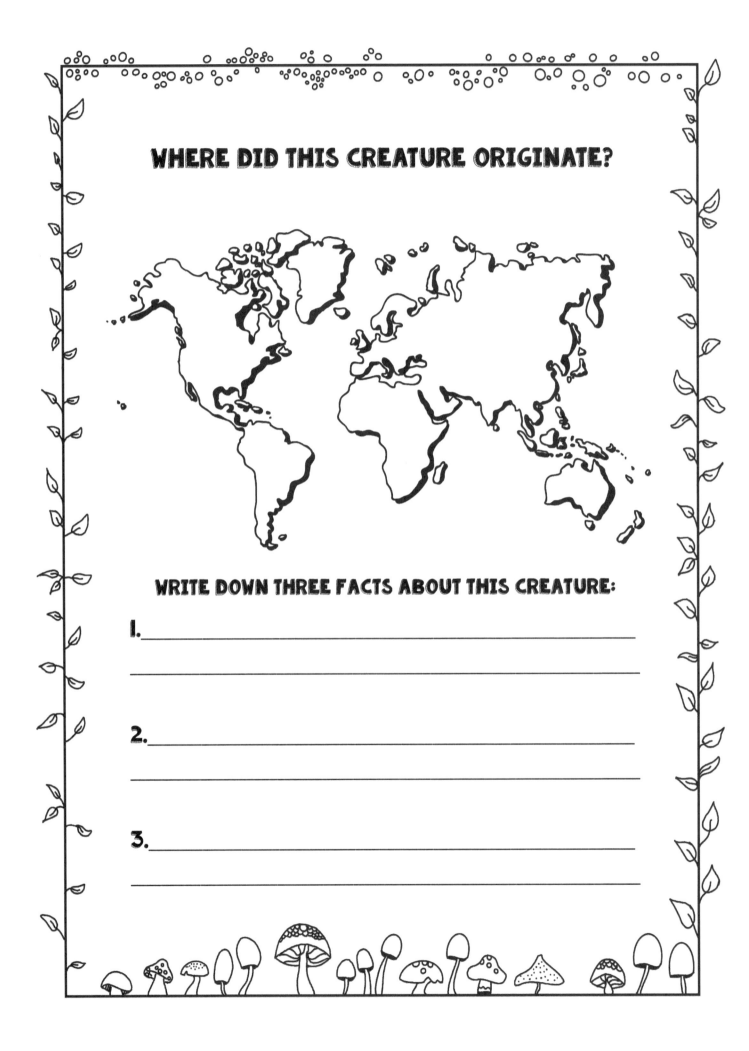

CAPRICORN

I am the oldest myth there is
I am half fish and half goat
I'm that bad guy in your stories
One of the worst you'll ever know

I might look sweet and quiet
But when the truth has been unfurled
You'll know my rage and greed
And my want to rule the world

But a goat cannot be king
At least that's what they said
So instead of ruling kingdoms
I rule your stars instead

I'm the king of constellations
You can find me in the night
And instead of bringing darkness
I bring you evening light

CREATIVE WRITING

Write a short story about this creature.

_____
_____
_____
_____
_____
_____
_____
_____
_____
_____
_____
_____
_____
_____
_____
_____

WHERE DID THIS CREATURE ORIGINATE?

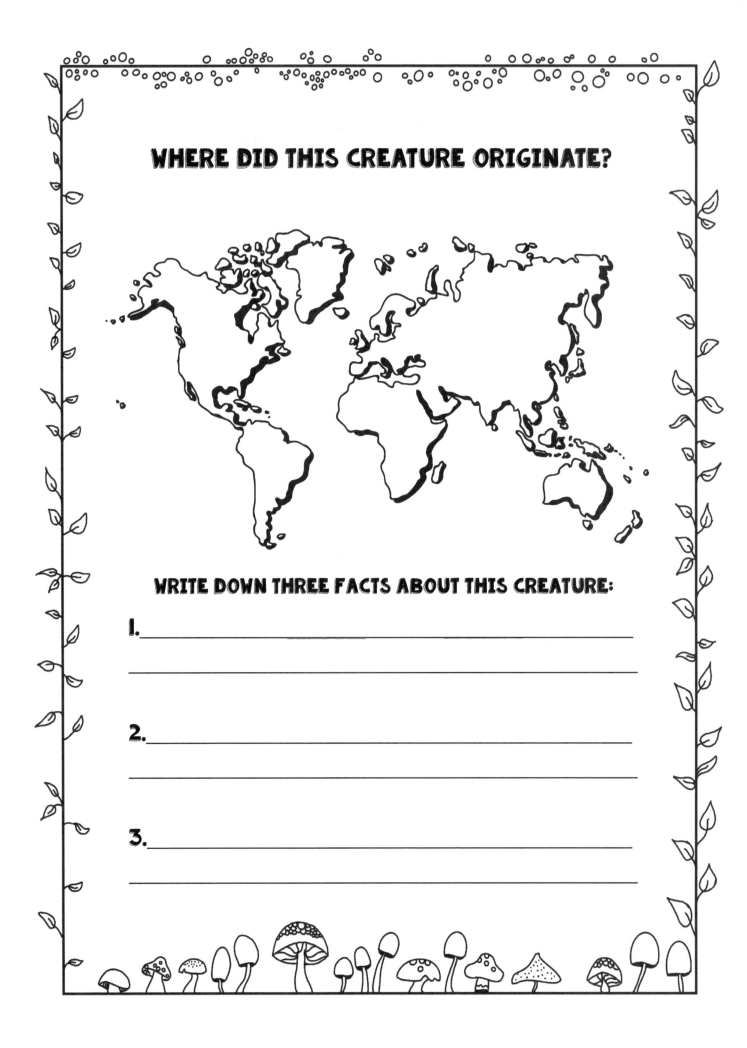

WRITE DOWN THREE FACTS ABOUT THIS CREATURE:

1._____
_____

2._____
_____

3._____
_____

ENFIELD

I am Enfield

Dragons and fairies exceed my popularity
Not many know my name
But I am a Celtic creature of wit, and strength
Loyalty, and honor

I watch over my people
As they fight for their cause
And when it's their time to fall
I, the Enfield, will rise
To guard them with my wings
And protect them with my claws

He who has lost his life
Should not also lose his honor
And now I shall fight on his behalf
Until his own can come and bury him

I am not well known among the living
But those who fought and risked it all
Your heroes
Know me well

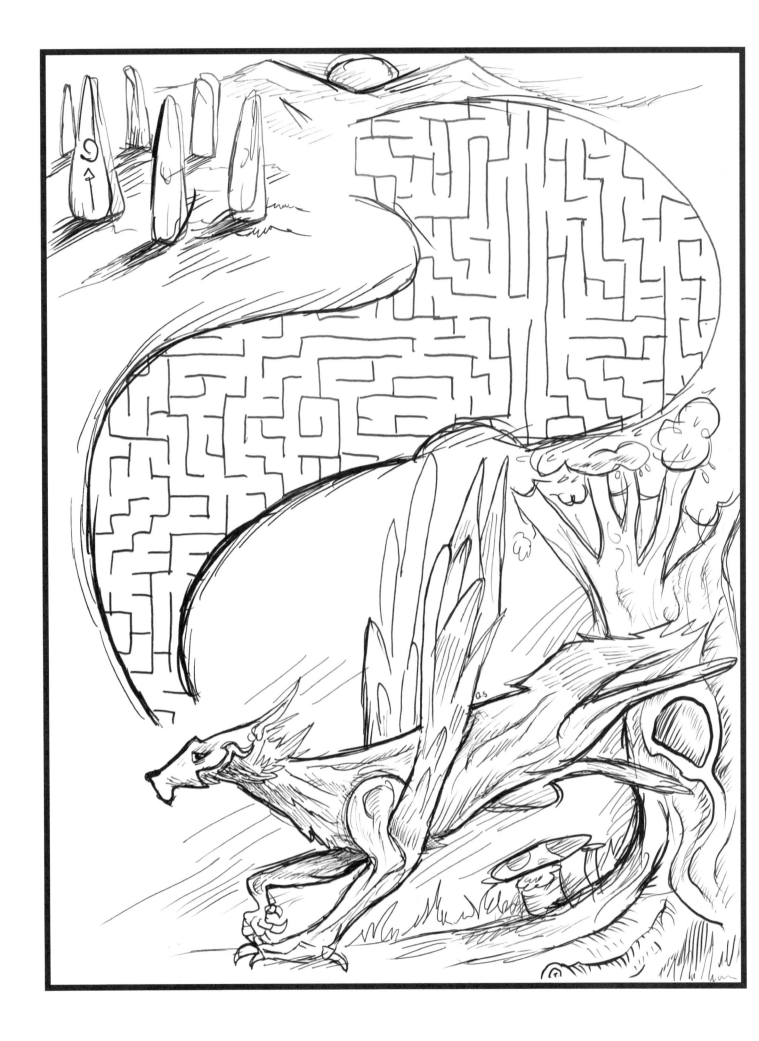

CREATIVE WRITING

Write a short story about this creature.

_____
_____
_____
_____
_____
_____
_____
_____
_____
_____
_____
_____
_____
_____
_____
_____
_____

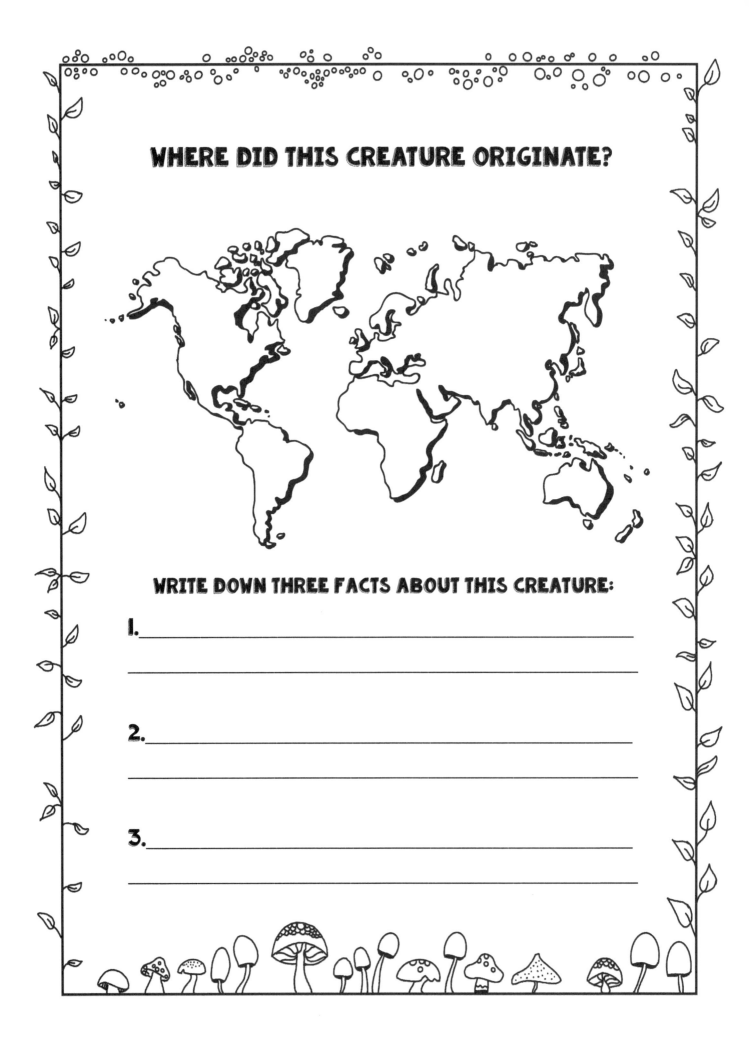

CYCLOPS

I am Brontes the cyclops!
Did you know my brothers and I?
We were trapped inside a dungeon
And we have no idea why!

But when we were free at last
We made lightning bolts for Zeus
You see, we're master blacksmiths
And we can be of much use

We made Poseidon's Trident
And other tools of war
And they say that our workshop
Would thunder, rumble, roar

And to get the little children
To sleep throughout the night
They said that the volcanoes
Were where we spent our nights

The volcanoes would not touch them
It was only cyclops three
My brothers, Steropes and Arges
Oh, and of course, me!

CREATIVE WRITING

Write a short story about this creature.

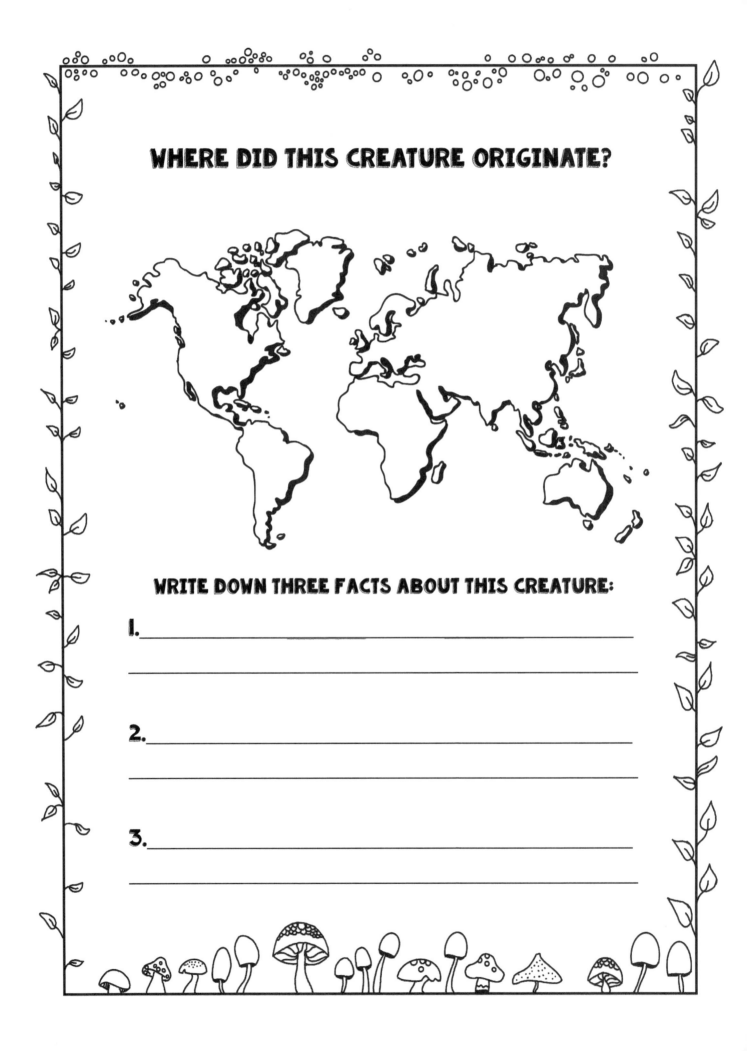

GNOME

Who am I? I am a gnome!
I make your garden feel like home!

I plant your flowers, feed your birds
And change the weather with my words

Your birds chirp, your flowers wake
And still you humans think I'm fake!

But just because you never see
Doesn't mean you can't believe

A gnome can be a mischievous one
If they don't have no garden to look upon

Please provide your very best,
a lovely place to live
And instead of taking to trouble-making
We gnomes will give, give, give!

CREATIVE WRITING

Write a short story about this creature.

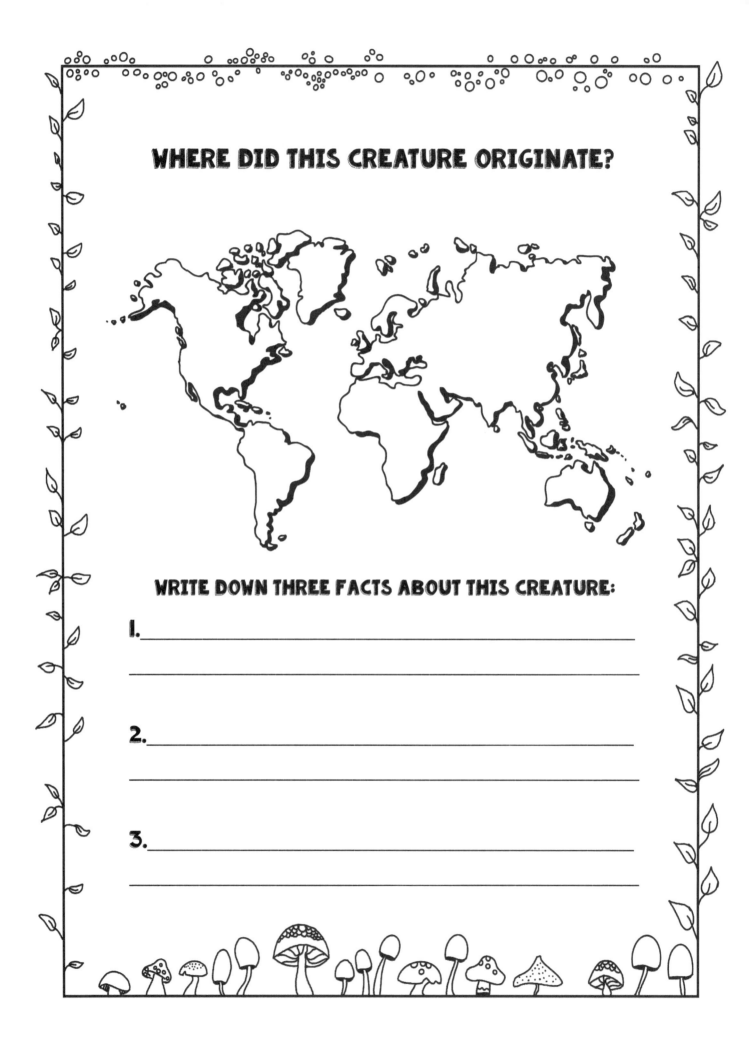

WHERE DID THIS CREATURE ORIGINATE?

WRITE DOWN THREE FACTS ABOUT THIS CREATURE:

1._____

_____

2._____

_____

3._____

_____

PIASA BIRD

Did you know there are three worlds?
Upperworld is heaven's bliss
Underworld is down below
And Thisworld is, well, this!

I am the Piasa Bird
And I help the three unite
I am not an evil one
And in attack I will take flight

I carry precious cargo
Not meant for thieving hands
I live along the river
I could not survive on land

It's harder now to hide
For less humans are my friends
I miss the days of old
With Native Americans

Who loved me as I was
Even though I appeared strange
They understood my purpose
And honestly, deep down inside
I wish things had stayed the same

WHERE DID THIS CREATURE ORIGINATE?

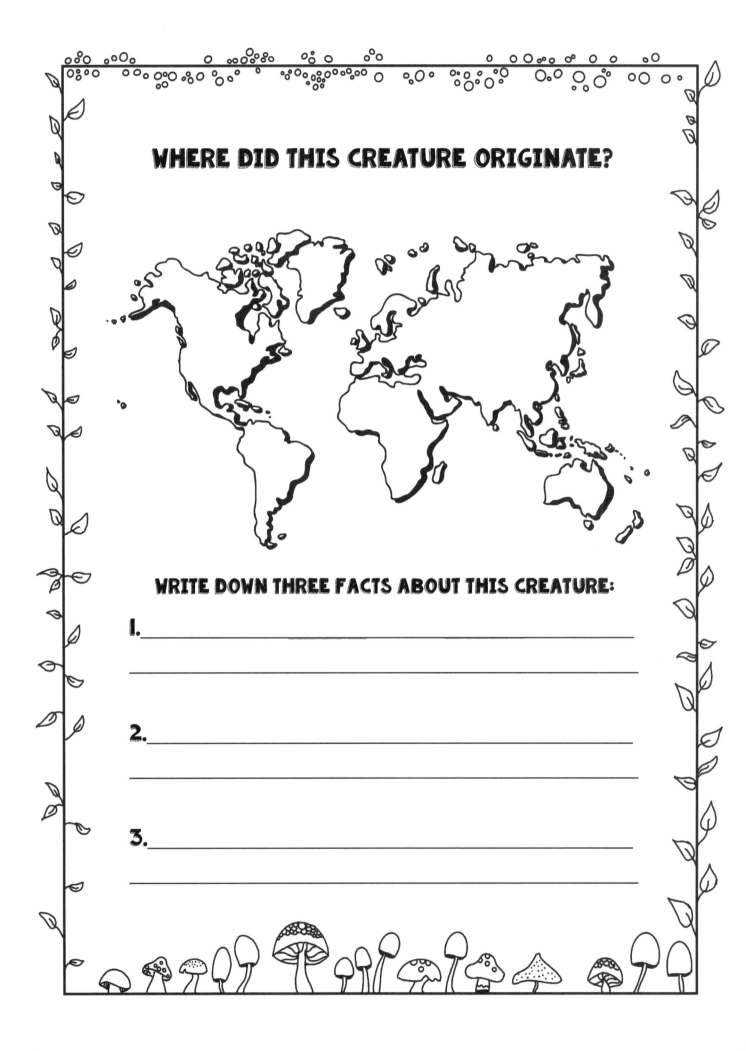

WRITE DOWN THREE FACTS ABOUT THIS CREATURE:

1._____
_____

2._____
_____

3._____
_____

FAIRY

We're the origins of Tinker Bell
We're magic, if you couldn't tell
The size of a thumb, but when we're born
We're only as big as a rosebush thorn

At the first laugh of a boy or girl
A dandelion fluff will lift and twirl
And catch the wind and quickly follow
The other seeds to Pixie Hollow

And certain fairies that we trust
Will come along with Pixie Dust
They'll sprinkle it upon the seedling
And bring a fairy into being

So the next time a dandelion comes your way
Be sure to blow the seeds away
To catch the laugh of girl or boy
Would be our pleasure, our utmost joy

We fairies view it as a mission
To bless each new and small creation

CREATIVE WRITING

Write a short story about this creature.

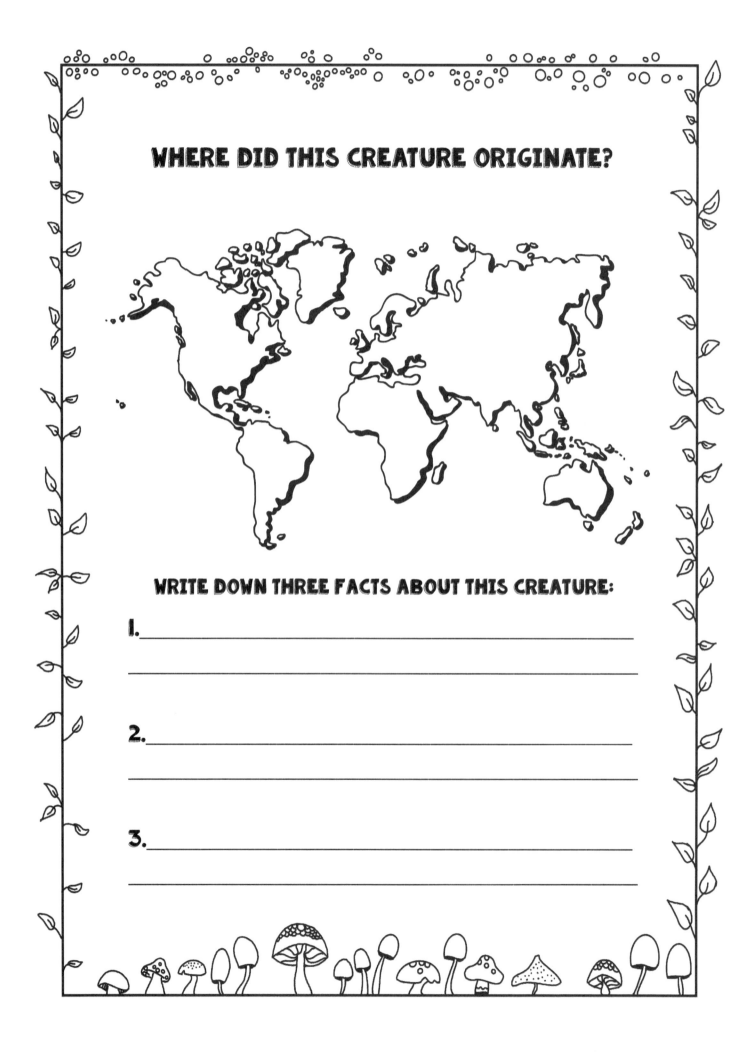

DRAGON OF WORMINSTER SLEIGHT

Call me fierce or terrifying
My daily acts are death-defying
As I feed on herds of sheep
Or snatch the cows when shepherds sleep

With twenty claws on four great legs
With dark green scales and deep brown eggs
I hide in moats and hills before attack
I wait 'till humans turn their backs

Oft' mistaken for a crocodile
My habits are more dark and vile
You can find art of me along Moat Walk
And of me the whole village talks

They call me ruthless, creepy, rude
Blame me for stealing, but a dragon needs food!
I am not tame, I've no respect
But I'm a *dragon*— what did you expect?

CREATIVE WRITING

Write a short story about this creature.

WHERE DID THIS CREATURE ORIGINATE?

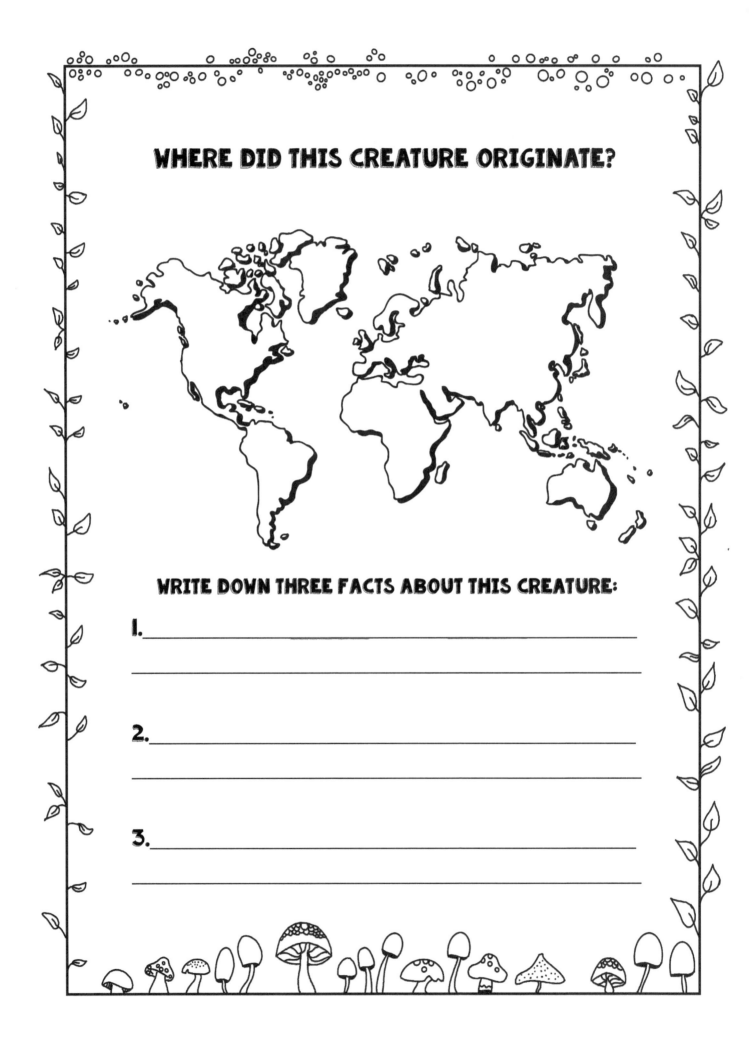

WRITE DOWN THREE FACTS ABOUT THIS CREATURE:

1._____
_____

2._____
_____

3._____
_____

MERMAID

I know I've heard of you
And I know you've heard of me
You're a child of the land
I'm the lady of the sea

I'm a scary myth to some
To others, a drama, full of glory
And some can't be convinced
Of any ancient story

You've seen me, heard me, known me
Yet you still demand
"then show me"
To the mermaids who've gone before me
And they've shown you time again

Every civilization in history
Has called me by my name
And whether I'm good or scary
I'm not starving for the fame

If you really truly seek me
And you respect that I am shy
And if you swim so boldly, deeply
Then a mermaid you shall find

CREATIVE WRITING

Write a short story about this creature.

_____
_____
_____
_____
_____
_____
_____
_____
_____
_____
_____
_____
_____
_____
_____
_____

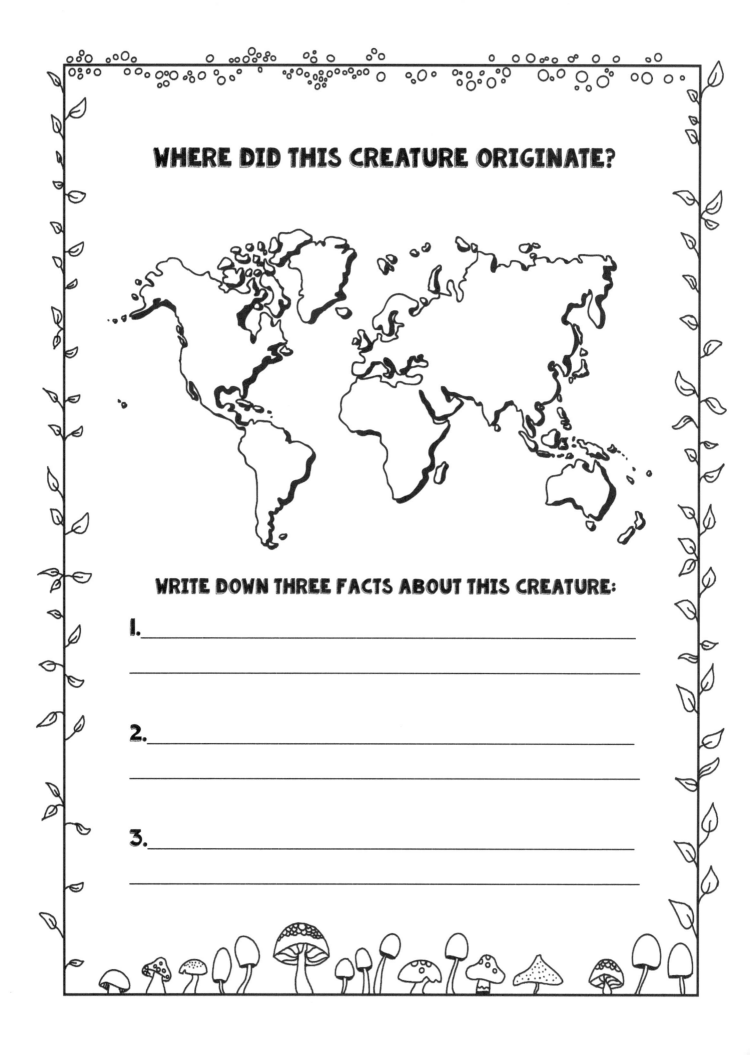

WHERE DID THIS CREATURE ORIGINATE?

WRITE DOWN THREE FACTS ABOUT THIS CREATURE:

1._____
_____

2._____
_____

3._____
_____

CENTAUR

I am seen in much Greek pottery
With horse and human half
Lived 'till I was old and tottery
And in old age, I'd pass

My sister was called a "centauress"
And did not even wear a dress!
Since, like a horse, we're clothed in hair
We have no need for underwear!

But we do, of course, put on a smile
And a shirt of the most modern style
We're smart and fun to the top degrees
Until we anger Hercules

Run circles 'round him, tease him so
In a dangerous game of run-and-hide
For to the forest we must go
If we all want to survive

CREATIVE WRITING

Write a short story about this creature.

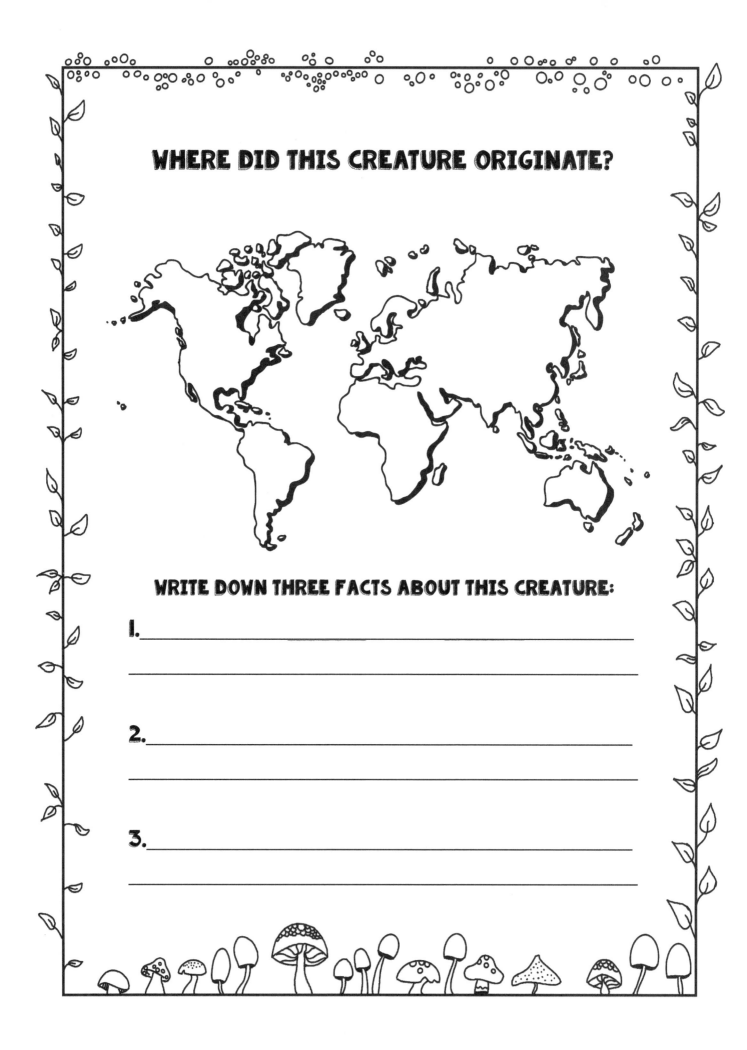

FAUN

Lover of sweet music
And protector of the wood
I am a Faun of Ancient Rome
I am not bad, but good

I've got only the best intentions
And if you cannot sleep at night
I'll bring my flute to calm you
And I'll make your sad heart bright

We care for every creature
When they're sick or hurt or lost
We give the fieldmice winter coats
To protect them from the frost

We make the brown grass green
We make the tall trees grow
We house rabbit families
And help the cool wind blow

We guard the wild with our flutes
In woods and mountainsides
You might never even find us
For we are always shy and hide
In the trees and caves and hollows
In holes and riversides

Just because we are not there
It doesn't mean we do not care
We're Fauns, with kindness and repute
And we guard the wild with our flutes

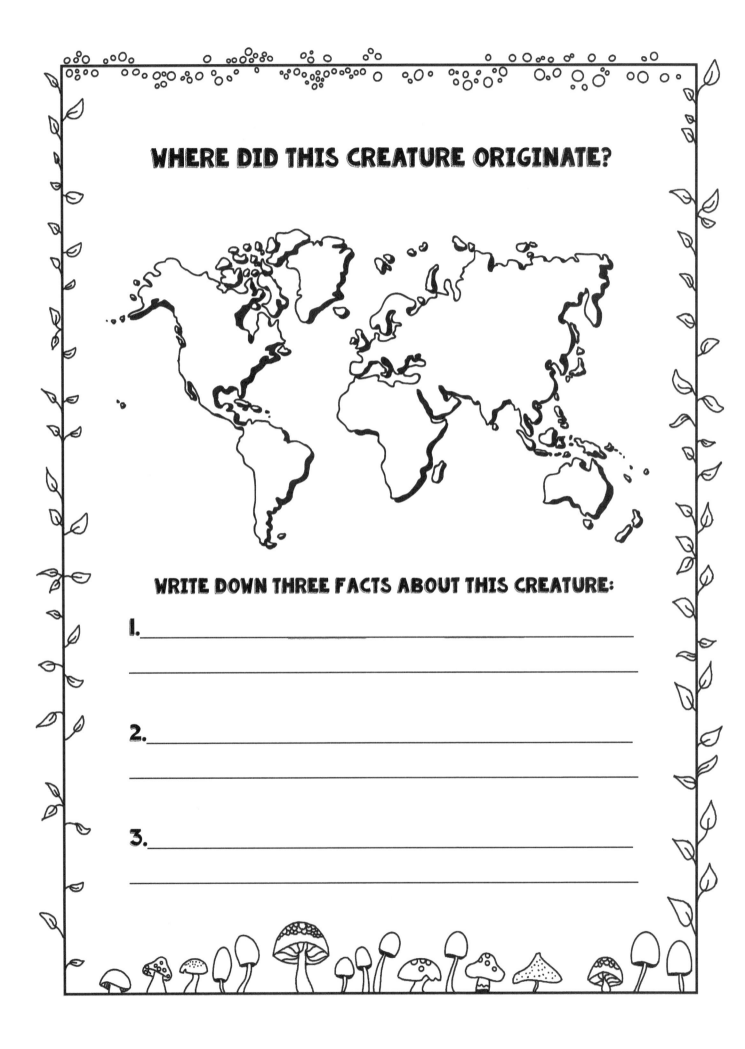

GRIFFIN

I'm a wise and honorable creature
In European tales of old
I've an eagle head with lion features
I guard precious jewels and gold

I'm a protective sort of animal
Across the sky I soar
Pulling chariots of fire
And fighting gods of war

I've yet to meet my match
And I'm the good guy you can trust
I bring calm and peace to villages
I turn enemies to dust

With my strength of a hundred steeds
And my wise and knowing eyes
I warn you not to stand up to me
Or you will meet your demise

And if you want to be my friend
And if your intentions are truly pure
I'd love to be your friend because
I've not had one before

CREATIVE WRITING

Write a short story about this creature.

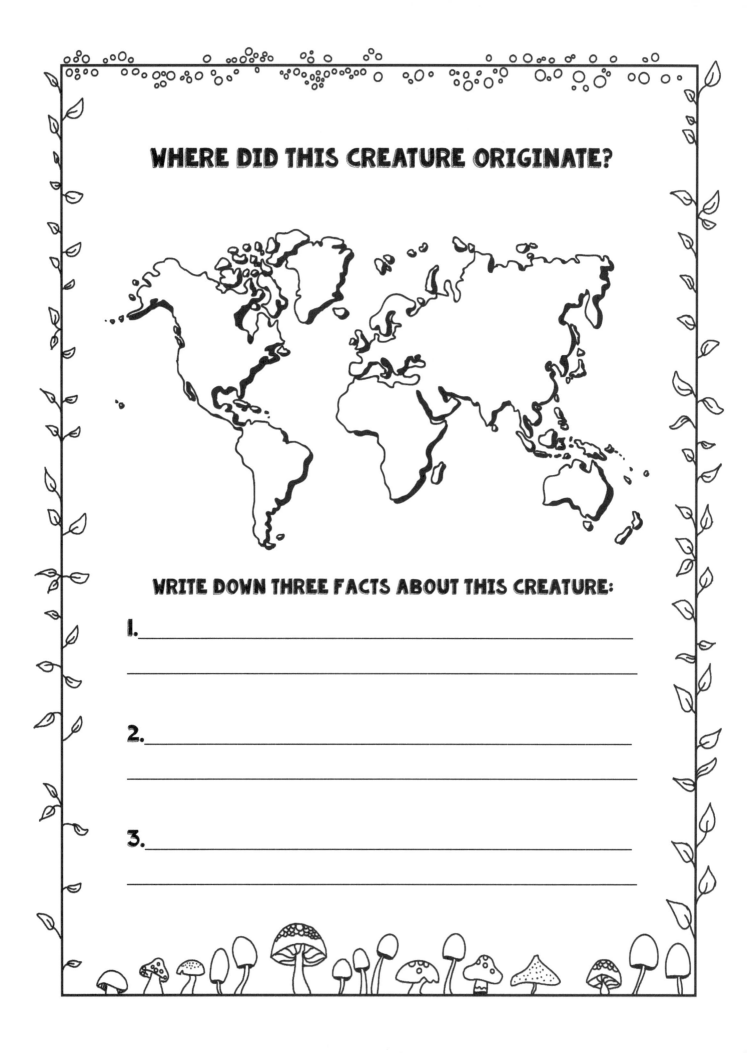

PHOENIX

I'm the legend of many origins
For I'm seen in many skies
You can try to pin me down but I
The fire bird, will always rise

Like a flame that blazes through the fields
Unstoppable in it's ways
I bring joy and happiness to you
And I will not be delayed

I'll travel through your countries
For a hundred thousand miles
And if you're having a hard day
I'll turn your frown into smile

And in a beautiful blurr
And with a mighty birdsong call
I'll bring happiness to humankind
'Till no more tears shall fall

CREATIVE WRITING

Write a short story about this creature.

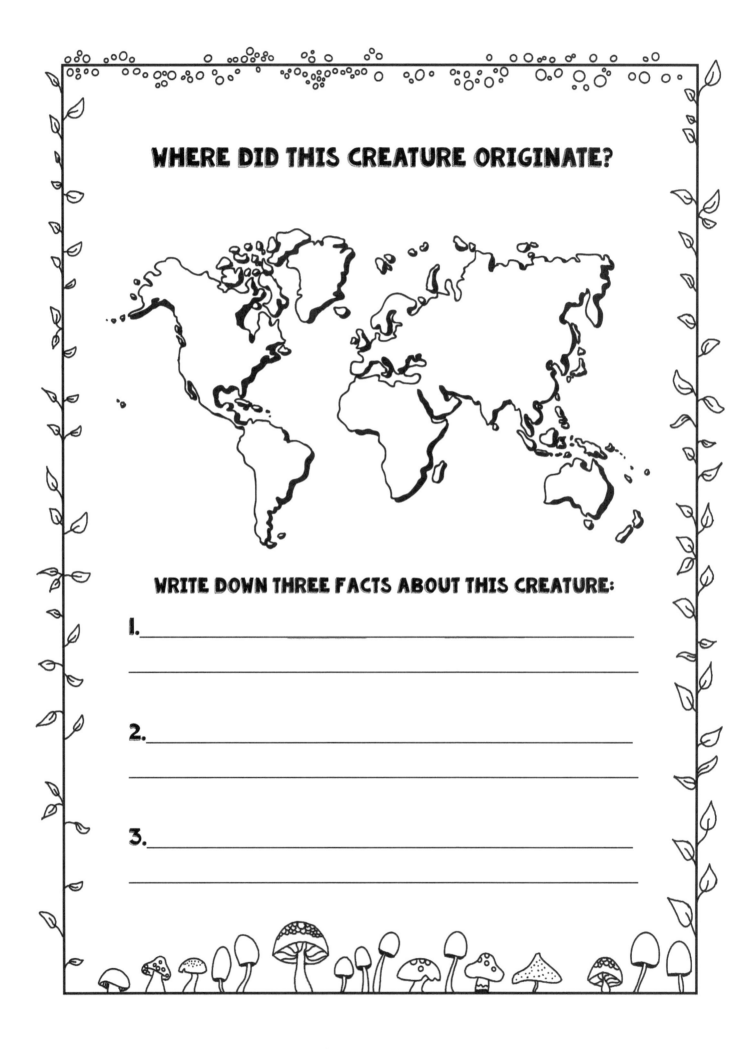

UNICORN

I'm the dream of every little girl
I'm the most colorful of steeds
I gallop through your picture books
And walk your myths with ease

There is no doubt about it
I'm the prettiest one of all
I'm elegant and colorful
And my horn makes me look tall

Paint rainbows in your bedrooms
Depict me in good light
I'm an endangered animal
Not of war, but flight

Hunters sought my magic horn
And royals sought my beauty
But I'd rather jump from sky high cliffs
Than be some trader's bounty

So draw me in your sketchbooks
Tell my stories of fame and glory
But for my safety, please, I beg you
Let me remain a story

CREATIVE WRITING

Write a short story about this creature.

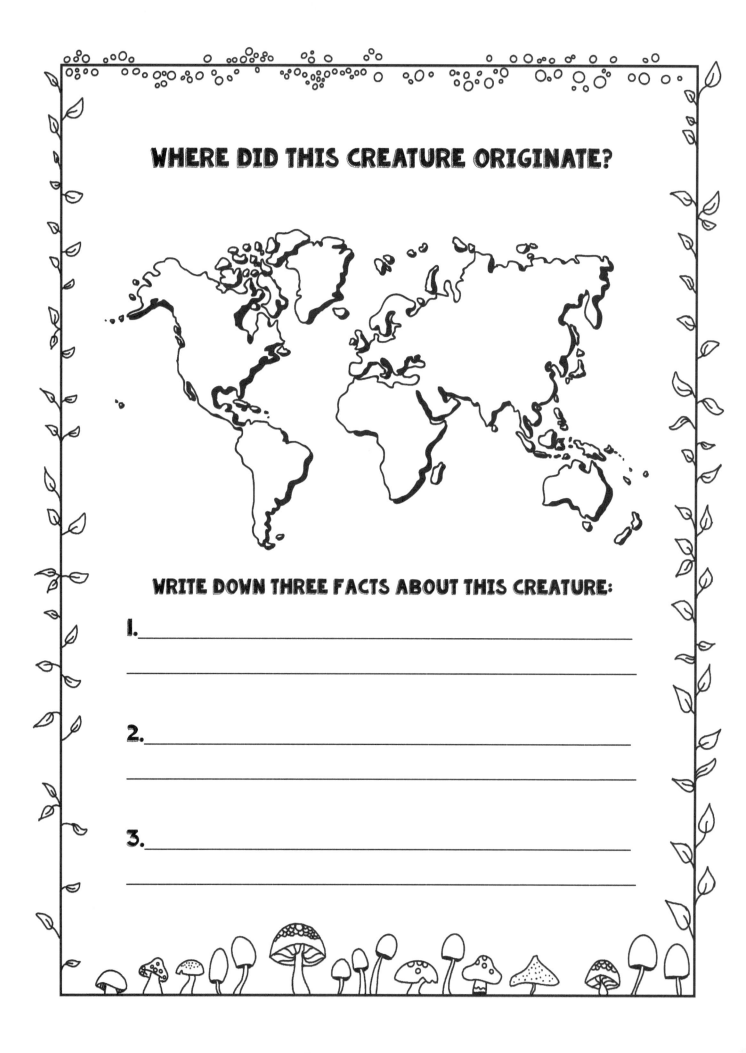

THE ELVES

The cousin of the fairy
And the magic of the land
I'm tiny, simple, merry
I plant gardens with my hands

The humming birds, they love me
The bees all like me too
And the sound of elves all humming
Means that they've got work to do

Turning all the soil over
Making room for newer plants
My friends all work together
And we do the best we can

To make the forest feel like home
So you always feel like you belong
No elf will ever work alone
We make sure that spring has sprung

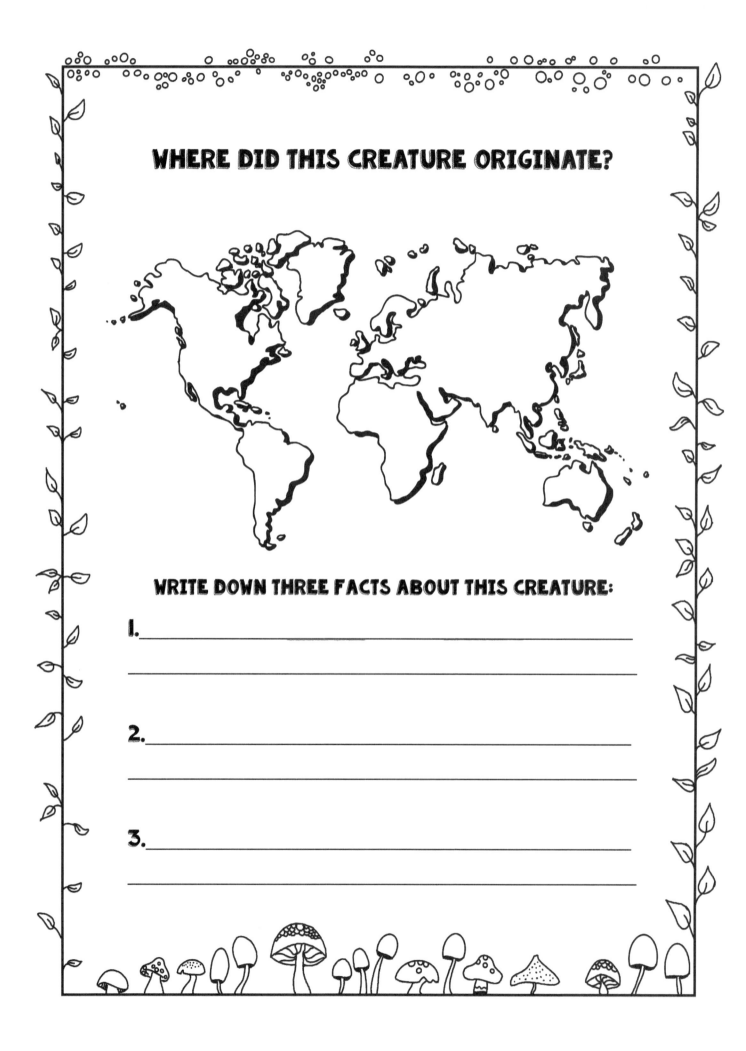

NYMPH

Hello, I am a Nymph!
My name is Babbling Brooke
You'll never ever find me
If you only stop to look

One must listen for a while
Cause mortals can only see me
But if you're feeling down
I can keep you company

If I like you well enough
I will sing you forest tunes
We can help the butterflies transform
And watch the flowers bloom

I can help you to be happier
I can take away your frown
I was the light of Greek mythology
And some say I'm still around

CREATIVE WRITING

Write a short story about this creature.

WHERE DID THIS CREATURE ORIGINATE?

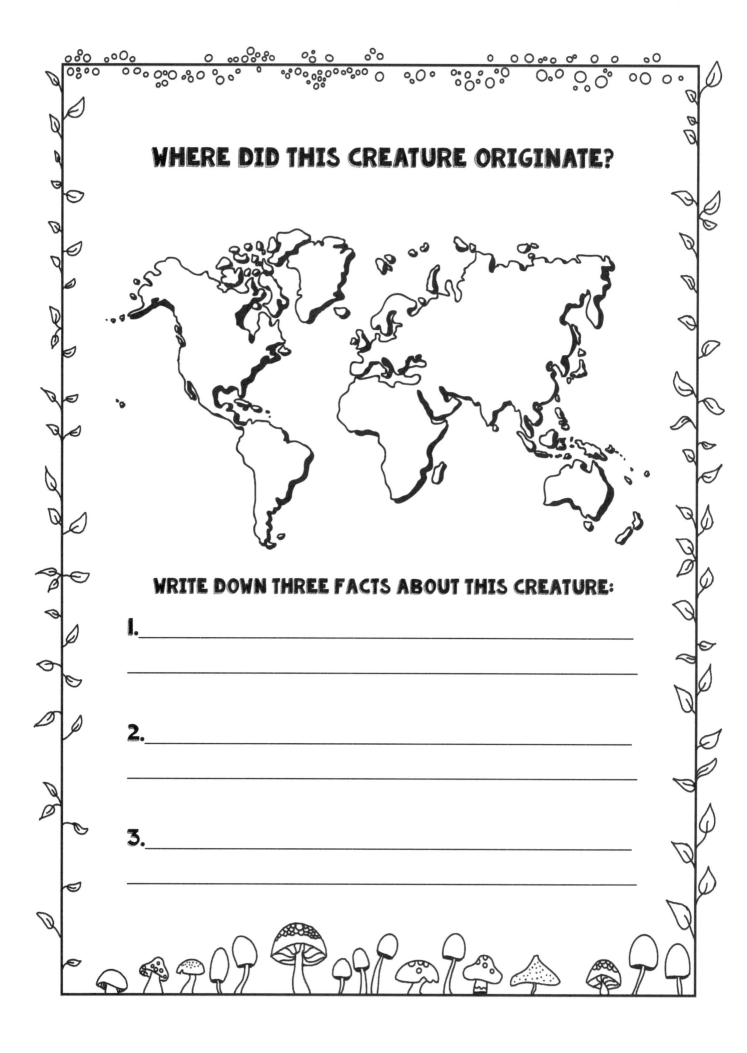

WRITE DOWN THREE FACTS ABOUT THIS CREATURE:

1._____
_____

2._____
_____

3._____
_____

PIXIE

I'm small but I am mighty
I can give you blessings new
But please don't make me angry—
I can give you curses too!

I can milk your cows and feed your flock
If I really aim to please
And I can make your day so sad and dark
You'll be begging on your knees

Ancient mythology made me
But it was the English who all shaped me
To the sweet and gentle Pixie
You all know me now to be

As long as my temper is not cross
And you bring me smiles, snacks and tea
I'll gladly bless your house
For all eternity

With little presents here
And an act of kindness or a kiss
Who wouldn't want a Pixie
If she gives you all of this!

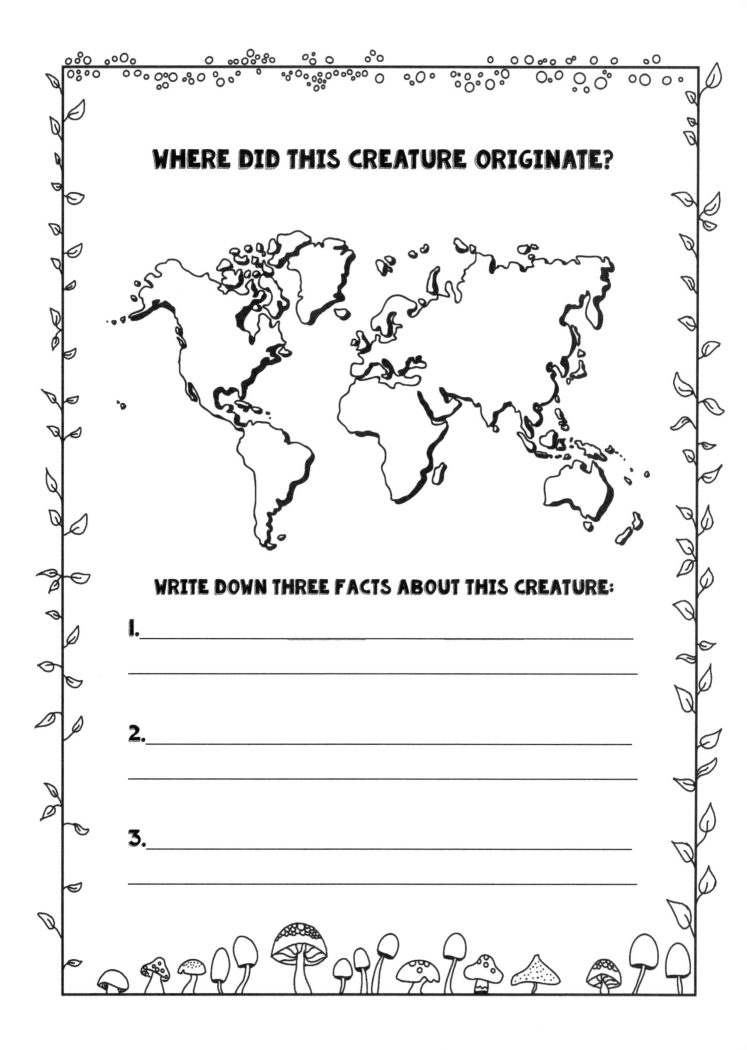

PEGASUS

To the Greeks I was creation
To the Asians I was a storm
I've been sprinkled in your stories
Since the moment I was born

Medusa is my mother
And Poseidon is my dad
I'm the most beautiful of offspring
An immortal could have had

I'm elegant and strong
I am beautiful and swift
These wings with long white feathers
Give my body lift

I'm the trusted steed of warriors
I carry souls to golden gates
I destroyed your biggest enemies
And changed the future's fate

I am mighty, I am calm
I'm intelligent and brave
And I will always watch the earthly beings
In search of souls to save

CREATIVE WRITING

Write a short story about this creature.

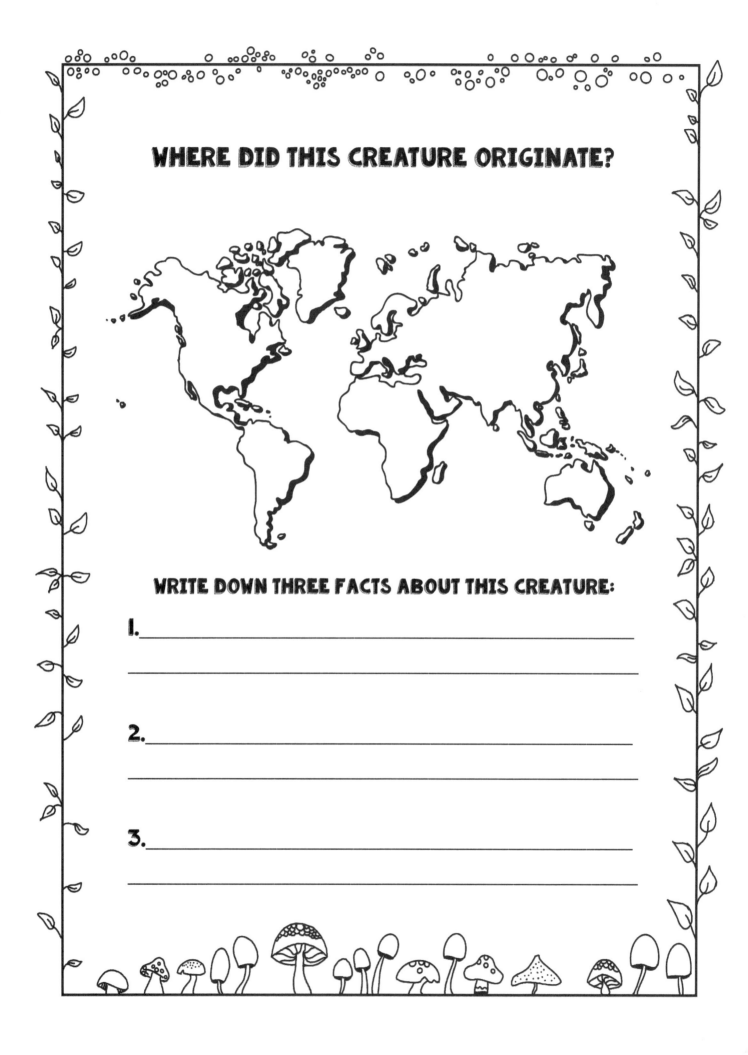

HYDRA

I was bred for love, affection
But raised for mass destruction
You may look upon me with disdain
But all I've known is pain

My mother didn't want me
And my father didn't care
Nine greedy heads grew on me
And no one realized they were there

Eighteen big eyes so hungry
For one gaze to look upon
The hurt and the neglect
That I had been raised on

They told you I'm a villain
The worst in all of Greece
Try to remove just one big head
And two others will take its place

You can't defeat me all alone
Not even Hercules
You cannot kill a dragon
With immortality

CREATIVE WRITING

Write a short story about this creature.

_____
_____
_____
_____
_____
_____
_____
_____
_____
_____
_____
_____
_____
_____
_____

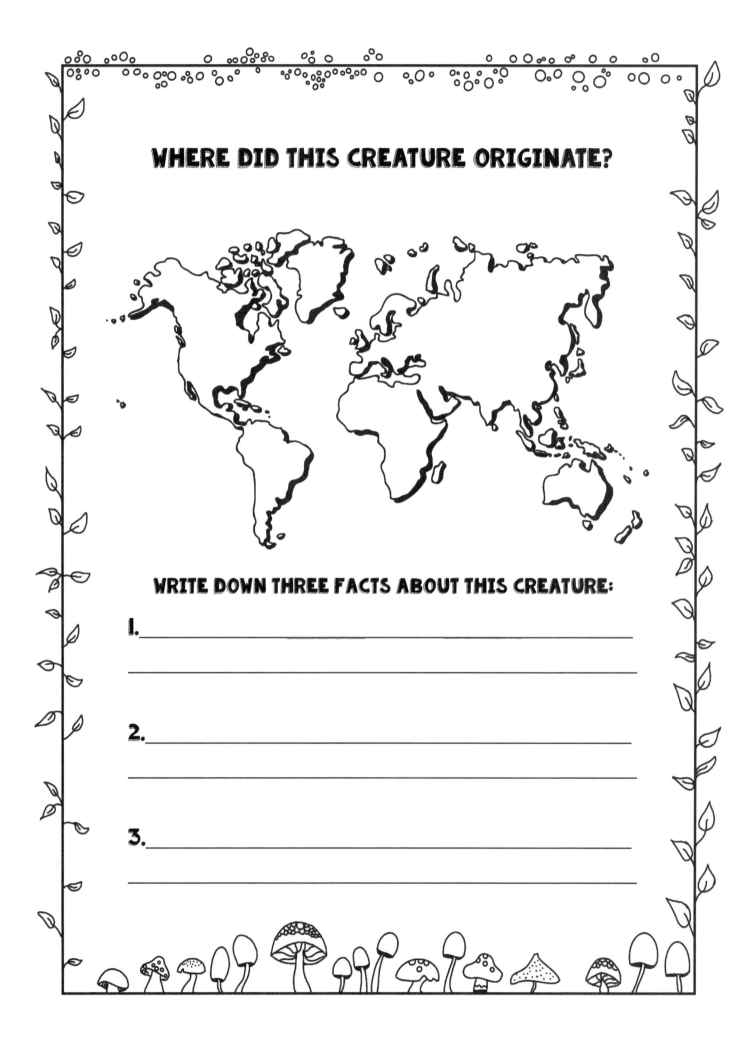

LEVIATHAN

My name is Leviathan
In the Bible, I've appeared
I am a symbol of the strength of God
I am a Serpent to be feared

I breathe fire from my nostrils
I'm covered in strong scales
Many did encounter me
Few lived to tell the tale

People have tried finding me
The water is my home
I'm a serpent of the sea
And I swim these depths alone

I make the mighty men look weak
And the brave men are afraid
The proud men become meek
And the non-believers pray

I'm the strongest one on earth
And no one dares boss me around
I don't think you want me lost
But I doubt you want me found

Because if you don't know where I am
That's a reason to be scared
But what's even more unsettling
Is knowing I am there

CREATIVE WRITING

Write a short story about this creature.

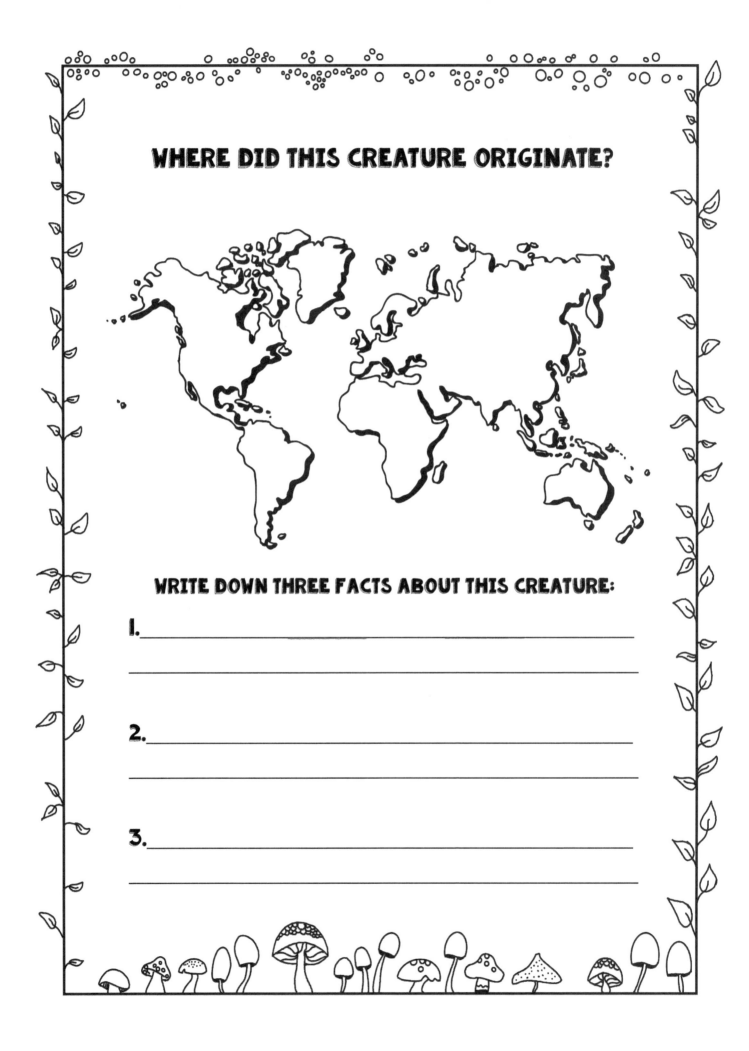

LONGMA

I can carry men, pull wagons
I can gallop, I can soar
In my name, "long", means dragon
And the last part, "ma", means horse

I emerged from the yellow river
Since before China began
And my presence means good things to come
To all my biggest fans

The emperors all knew me
For I came as often as one can
And fortune passed right through me
To bring wealth to every man

Many label me a Pegasus
But I'll tell you, I'm no such thing
Just because I am a horse
With mighty, graceful wings
In the sea, the sky, and land

Is a Pegasus a dragon?
They can't measure up to me!
And I've never known a Pegasus
To live in rivers, lakes and seas

No, I am a Longma
And you'll treat me as I am
The best and kindest dragon
In the sea, the sky, and land

DRAW THIS CREATURE:

CREATIVE WRITING

Write a short story about this creature.

_____
_____
_____
_____
_____
_____
_____
_____
_____
_____
_____
_____
_____
_____
_____
_____
_____

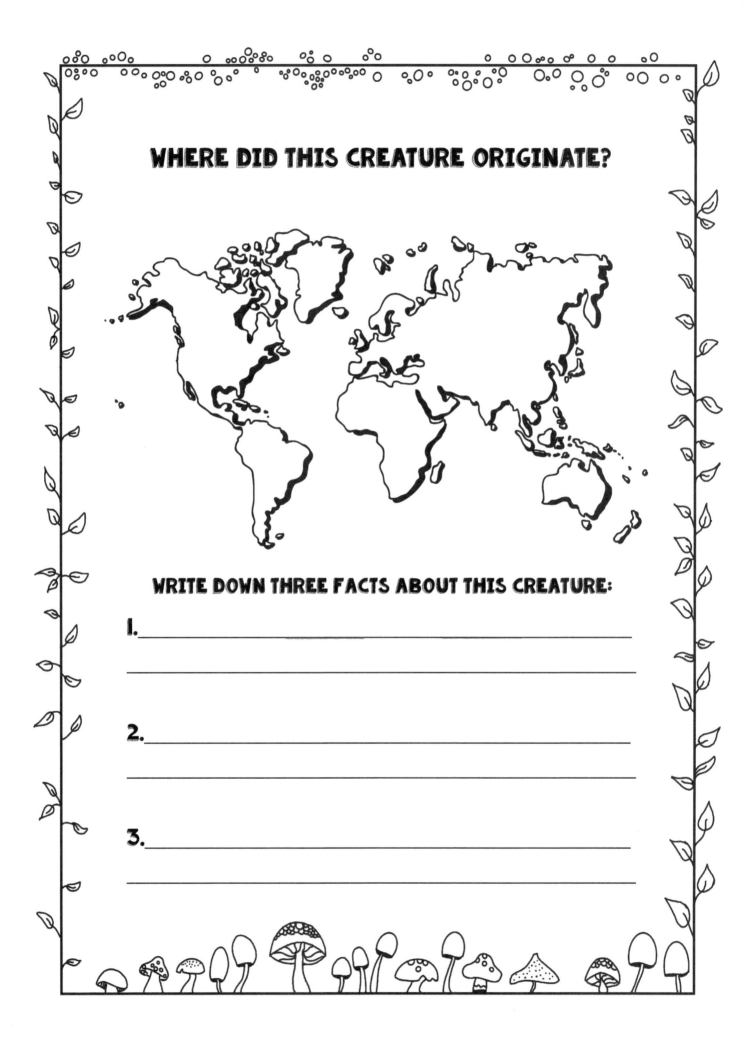

AFRICAN RAINBOW SERPENT

I'm an African Rainbow Serpent
You can call me Dan
I know that name is funny
Look it up— it's who I am!

I'm the deity of rainbows
Of serpents young and old
I'm the goddess of fertility
And my coloring is bold

My scales are iridescent
Do you know what that word means?
My colors change with angles
But my scales will always gleam

I have a heart for wisdom
And I have an eye for love
I have an ear to listen
From my branches up above

Bring me offerings of milk and rice
For I am so pure and clean
If you do, I'm said to bless you
With peace and integrity

CREATIVE WRITING

Write a short story about this creature.

_____
_____
_____
_____
_____
_____
_____
_____
_____
_____
_____
_____
_____
_____
_____
_____

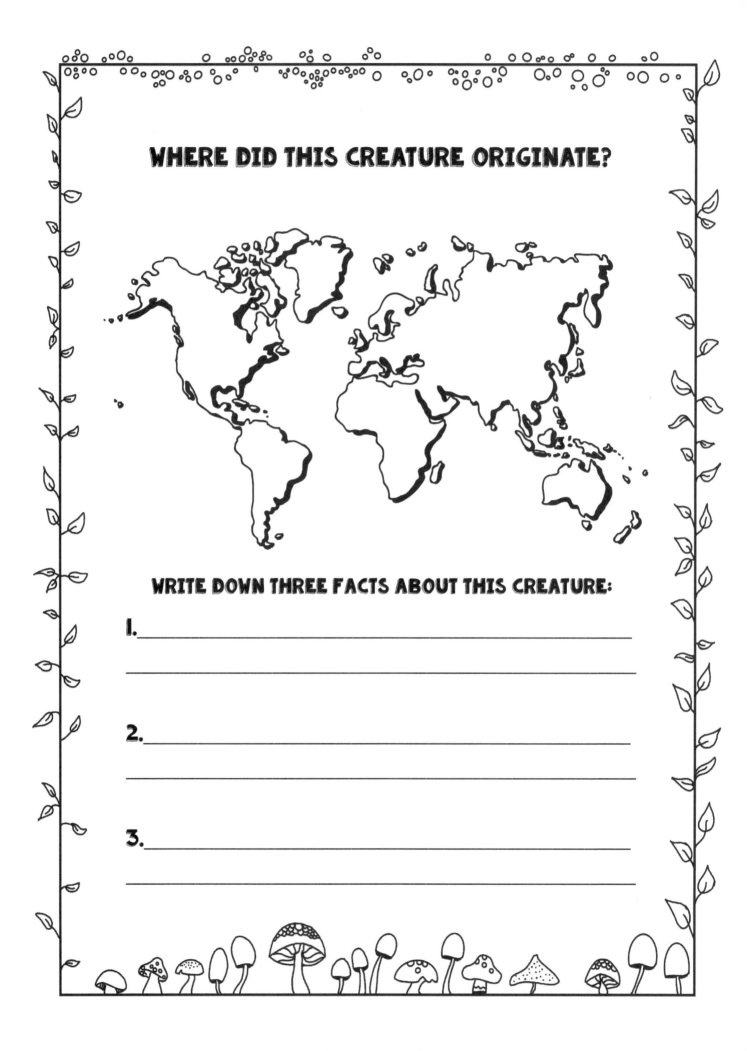

KITSUNE

Hi, my name is Chaos
And I'm very, very sly
Can you count my nine long tails
As I go whizzing by?

I cause trouble every day
And I make my parents mad
But you have no need to worry
Kitsunes are not always bad

We grow to be protectors
And defenders of the land
When we're young we cause more trouble
Than all the children of Japan

We convince you with our trickery
And deceive you with our eyes
We can cause a world of trouble
With our shapeshifting disguise

But as adults, we'll work with you
To keep you safe and sound
You'll never have to worry
When the Kitsunes are in town

CREATIVE WRITING

Write a short story about this creature.

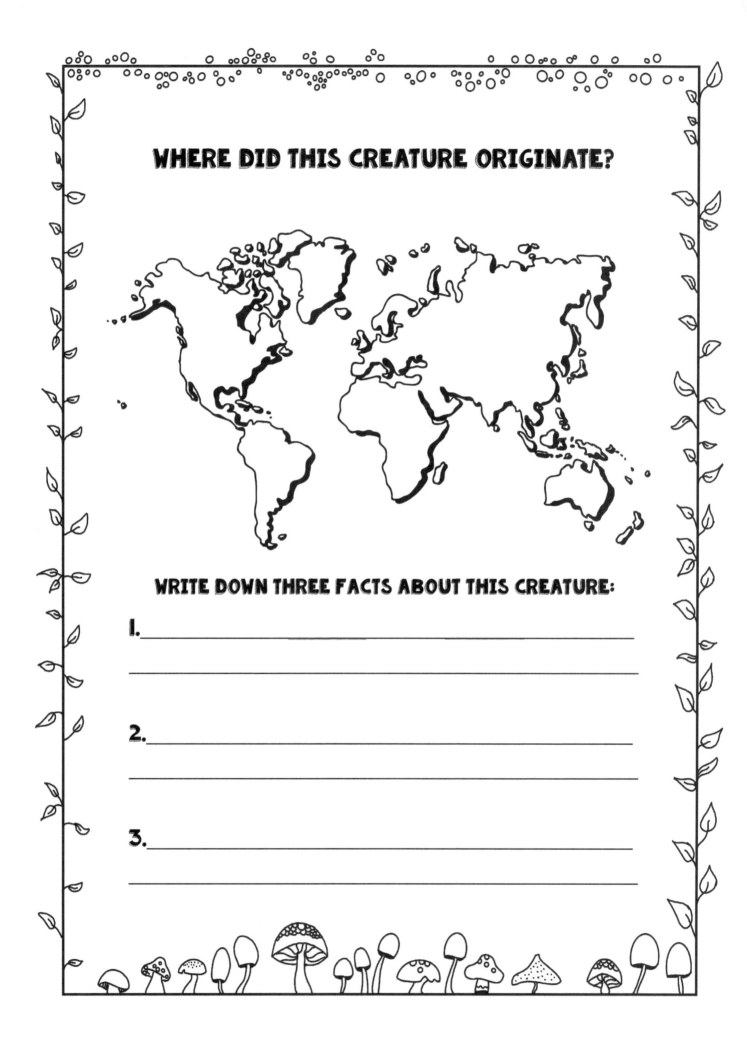

MIDGARD WYRM

I am a Sea Serpent at large!
And you'll never, ever find me
I'm a criminal you cannot charge
For Midgard doesn't mind me

As long as I don't show my face
You humans do not care
But to Odin I am a disgrace
And it simply isn't fair

Who cares that I've grown big and strong
And I've got trouble in my eyes
True, you would never last that long
'Fore you met your demise

I have no hands for holding
Not touchy-feely in the least
But I would gladly wrap around you
If you would kindly be my feast

And perhaps that's why they're after me
Now that I think about it
I should probably not talk so loud
Odin might not allow it

And he'll be after me, I'm sure
To save me from the earth
He's been doing so since the very day
My mother gave me birth

DRAW THIS CREATURE:

CREATIVE WRITING

Write a short story about this creature.

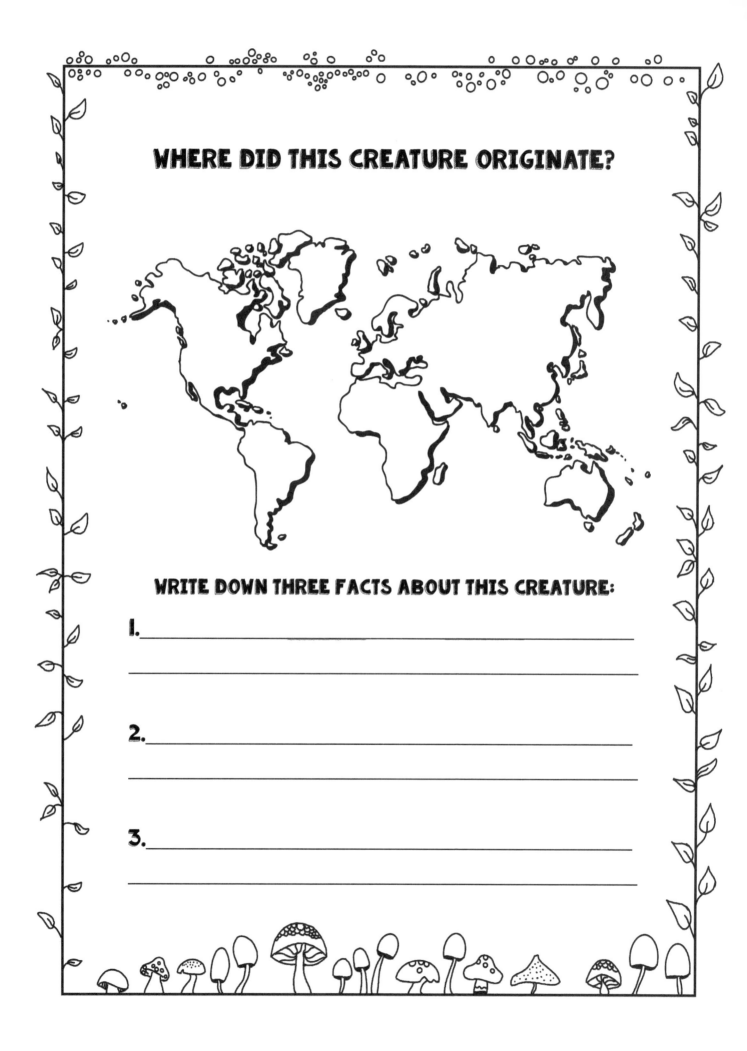

WHERE DID THIS CREATURE ORIGINATE?

WRITE DOWN THREE FACTS ABOUT THIS CREATURE:

1._____
_____

2._____
_____

3._____
_____

CERBERUS

Look at me! And what am I?
I'm a three headed dog!
I have one giant body
And my heads don't get along

Hide behind that tree
And don't forget to throw three bones
For if I look upon you
You will be turned to stone

I'm the watchdog of the underworld
So if you misbehave
You might find me guarding after you
Beyond your earthly grave

I want to be much nicer
And guard the golden gates
But the goodness of my character
Is under much debate

Am I just a myth?
Or is what I'm saying true?
If Heaven needs its angels
Then they might need guard dogs, too

And look at me, a three-in-one!
Who couldn't pass this deal!
And plus, you see, I come pre-trained
I know come, and sit, and heel

DRAW THIS CREATURE:

DRAW THE MISSING PARTS

CREATIVE WRITING

Write a short story about this creature.

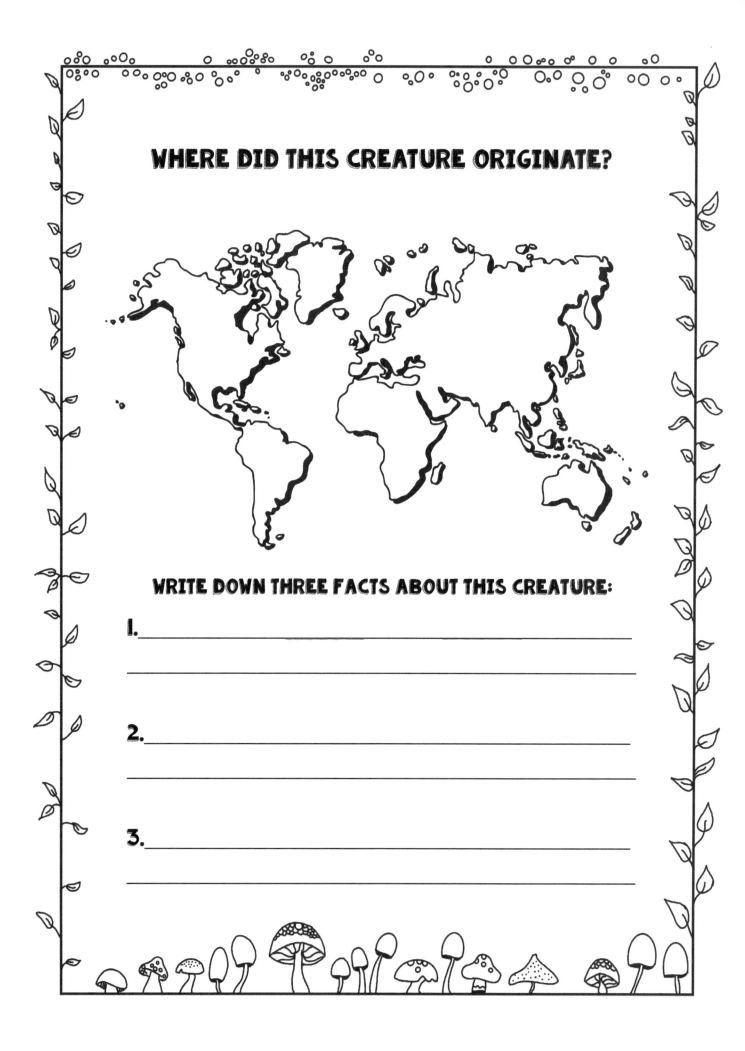

ORIENTAL DRAGON

I am a Chinese dragon
Oriental is my name
I have no idea when I was born
But from myths I know I came

I'm the most ancient emblem
That anybody knows
I breathe fire from my nostrils
My teeth have many rows

I tell the stars when to rise
And the moon when it's her turn
I make the clouds rain down on you
I make the sunshine burn

I have a bunch of scales
A hundred seventeen
I am strong and muscular
And I am swift and lean

I know not a single flying thing
Is a better one than I
For they all require wings
But I don't need them to fly

I'm so popular and pretty
You never can forget
I'm the oriental dragon
And my beauty is unmet

CREATIVE WRITING

Write a short story about this creature.

WHERE DID THIS CREATURE ORIGINATE?

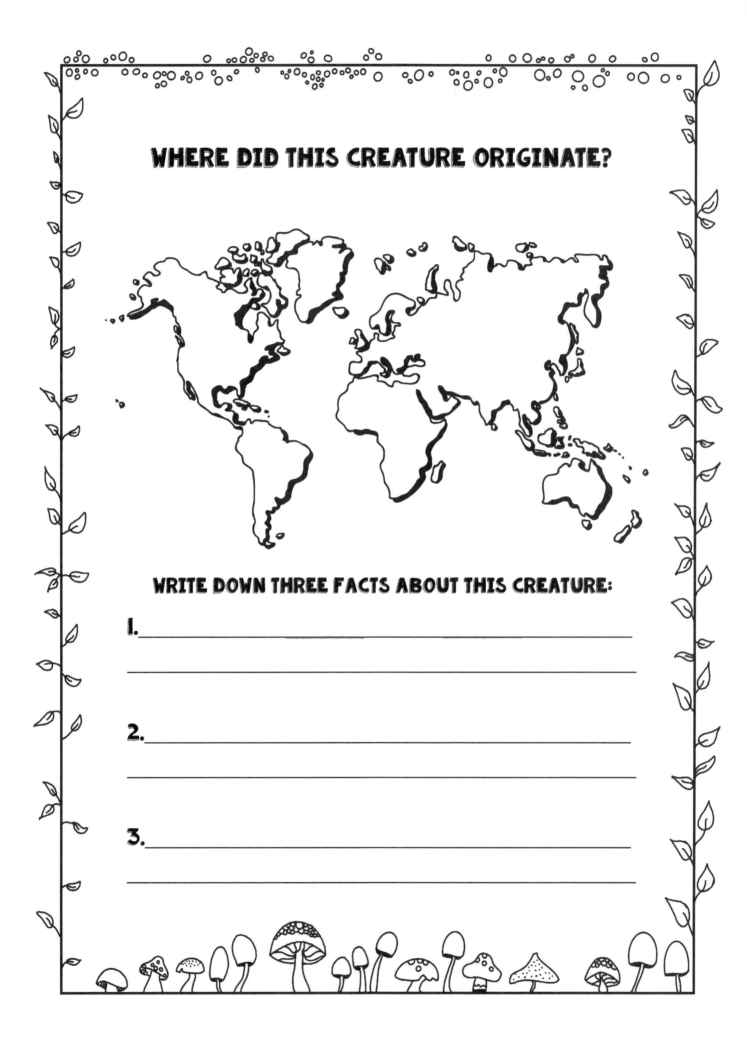

WRITE DOWN THREE FACTS ABOUT THIS CREATURE:

1._____

_____

2._____

_____

3._____

_____

NEMEAN LION

I'm the lion of Nemea
I am strong but hate the fight
I'm not an animal of hunt
When hunted, I take flight

But many thought me mighty
For you couldn't pierce my skin
I became a fearsome predator
But I never aimed to win

My fur was just so crazy thick
It broke arrows, swords and knives
I became a challenger
When I just wanted to live my life

So because of reputation
I became wild, cruel and mean
Some wisdom I can give you
I wish someone had told me

Life will give you thicker skin
To protect your heart inside
But in a world so full of sin
It's impossible to hide

Show your feelings, take the risk
Don't let your thick skin be a wall
Let others see your weaknesses
Learn to love the fall

And maybe you can teach the world
To be kind and good and true
Just a few small words of wisdom
I wish someone told me too

DRAW THIS CREATURE:

CREATIVE WRITING

Write a short story about this creature.

_____
_____
_____
_____
_____
_____
_____
_____
_____
_____
_____
_____
_____
_____
_____
_____
_____

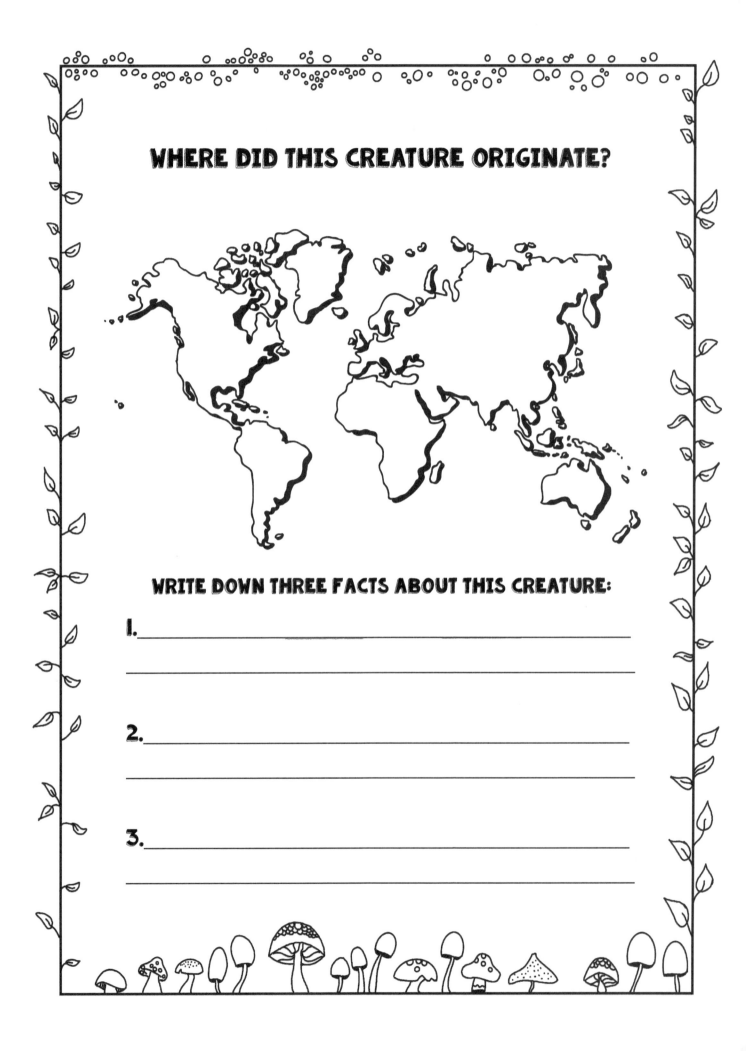

BISTERNE DRAGON

I started out so nice and calm
No one could have guessed
That a dragon as kind and wise as me
Could be anything but the best

And you gave me gifts of milk each day
And, while I thank you for all that
I couldn't help but noticing
Those sheep so round and fat

One day my hungry stomach
Became too much for milk to feed
So I borrowed but one ewe from you
And I developed *greed*

Such a feeling to be greedy
One all good dragons hate
But me, I quite enjoyed it
So I ate, and ate...
And ate...

CREATIVE WRITING

Write a short story about this creature.

WHERE DID THIS CREATURE ORIGINATE?

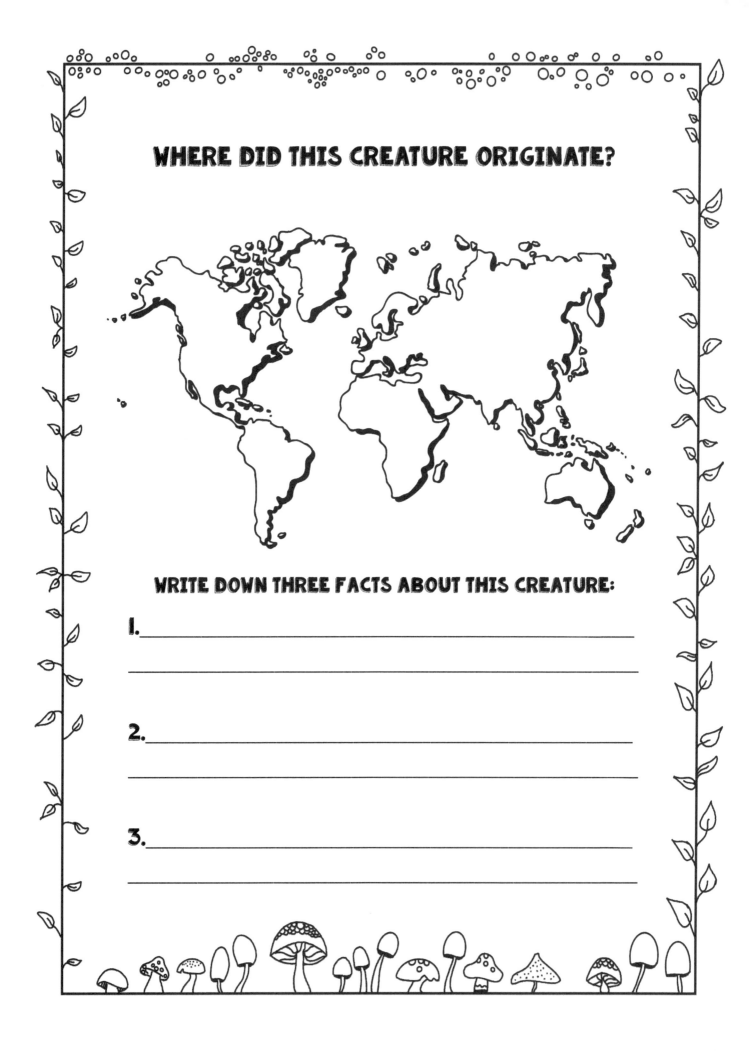

WRITE DOWN THREE FACTS ABOUT THIS CREATURE:

1._____
_____

2._____
_____

3._____
_____

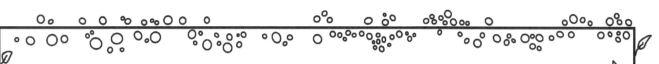

FANTASY DRAGON

From the beginning of time, until now
People tell stories, their fantasy
They create the when and why and how
The creation of creatures like me

Sometimes because of something they've seen
The creation that's already there
They'll make dragons like me
With legs or with wings
With scales or feathers or hair

And our stories take shape, take form, take off
Until we're as real as your wildest dreams
Soaring through the sky
And take form as the generations go by
Some truer than others
But all invention of mind

And at last, at the end of the day
The best creature that anyone could ever design
Look in the mirror—it's you and it's me
And all the people ever to be
The best creatures are humankind

CREATIVE WRITING

Write a short story about this creature.

DESIGN YOUR OWN CREATURE!

_____

(NAME)

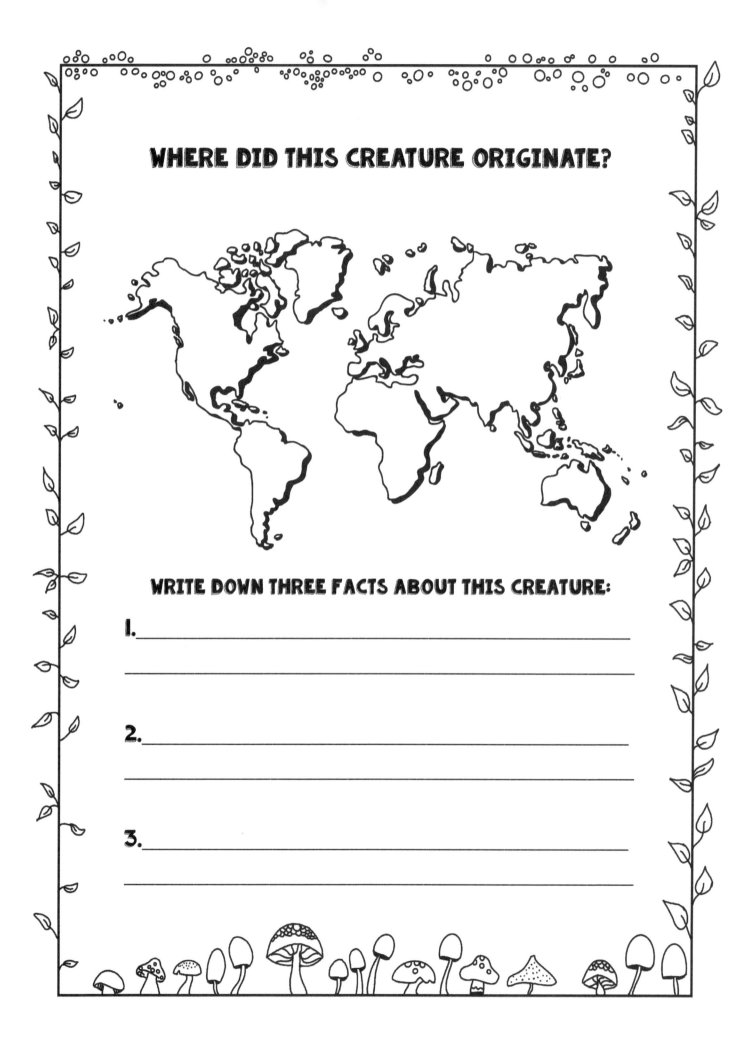

DESIGN YOUR OWN CREATURE!

_____

(NAME)

WRITE YOUR POEM:

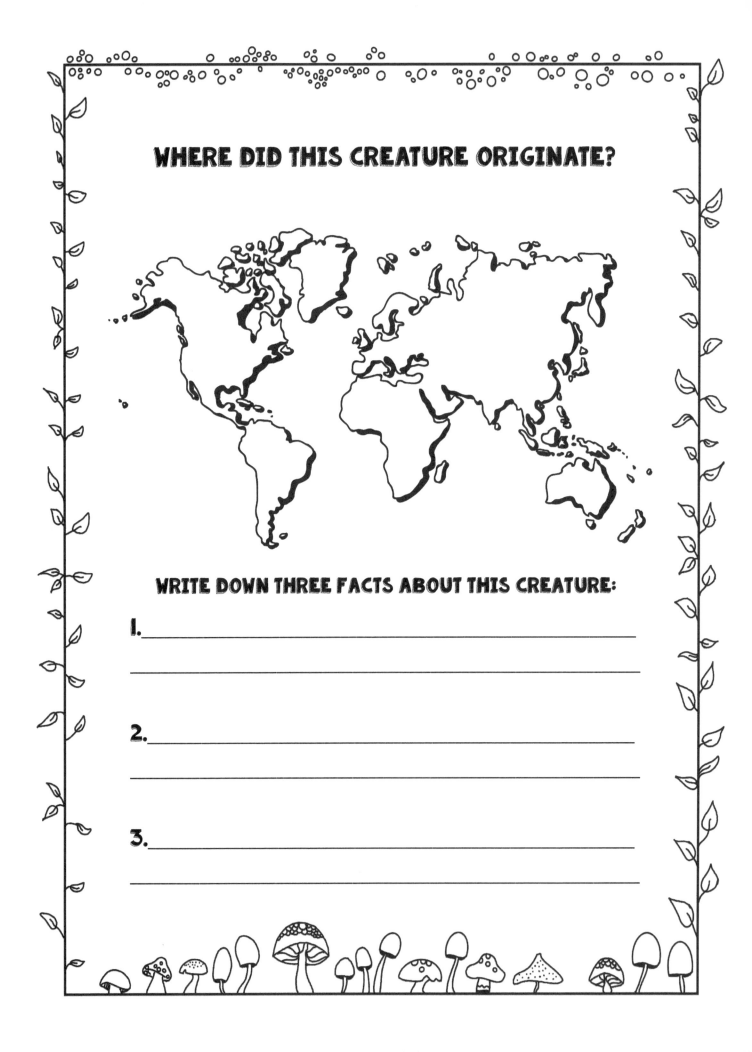

DESIGN YOUR OWN CREATURE!

_____

(NAME)

WRITE YOUR POEM:

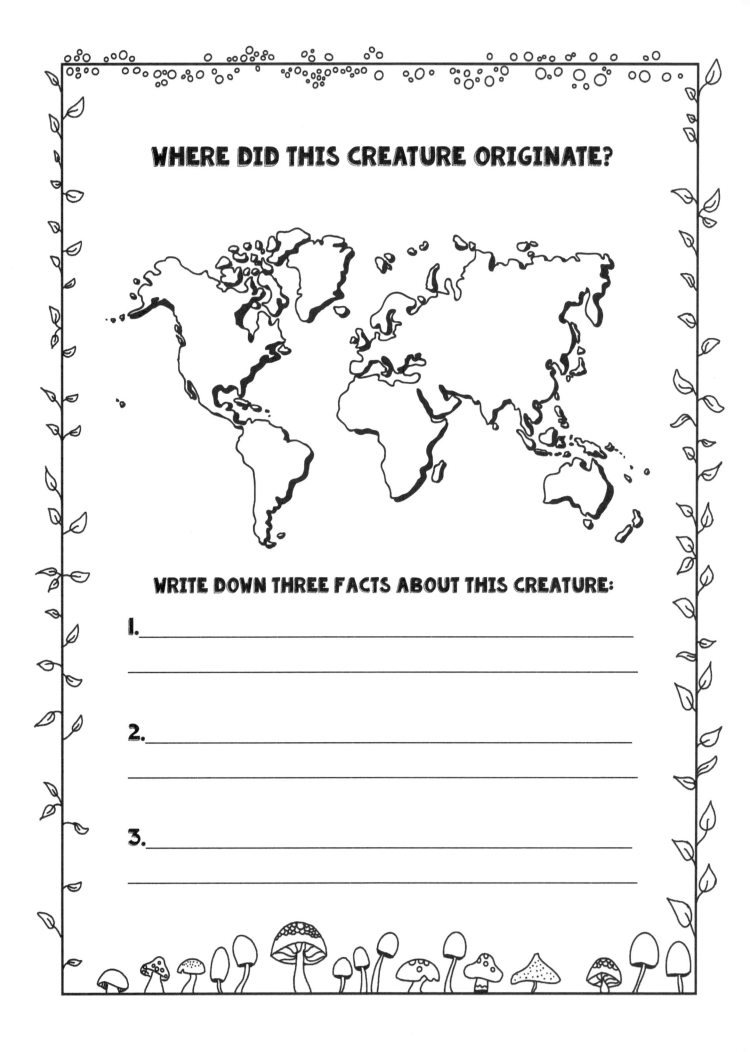

WHERE DID THIS CREATURE ORIGINATE?

WRITE DOWN THREE FACTS ABOUT THIS CREATURE:

1. _____

2. _____

3. _____

Made in United States
Troutdale, OR
04/15/2024

19192727R00137